Civil Procedure in South Africa

Civil Procedure in South Africa

Fourth Edition

Roshana Kelbrick
Fawzia Cassim

This book was originally published as a monograph in the International Encyclopaedia of Laws/Civil Procedure.

Founding Editor: Roger Blanpain
General Editor: Frank Hendrickx
Volume Editor: Piet Taelman

Wolters Kluwer

Published by:
Kluwer Law International B.V.
PO Box 316
2400 AH Alphen aan den Rijn
The Netherlands
E-mail: international-sales@wolterskluwer.com
Website: lrus.wolterskluwer.com

Sold and distributed in North, Central and South America by:
Wolters Kluwer Legal & Regulatory U.S.
7201 McKinney Circle
Frederick, MD 21704
United States of America
Email: customer.service@wolterskluwer.com

Sold and distributed in all other countries by:
Air Business Subscriptions
Rockwood House
Haywards Heath
West Sussex
RH16 3DH
United Kingdom
Email: international-customerservice@wolterskluwer.com

Printed on acid-free paper

ISBN 978-94-035-0294-6

e-Book: ISBN 978-94-035-0165-9
web-PDF: ISBN 978-94-035-0263-2

Printed in the United Kingdom.

The Authors

Roshana Kelbrick is a former Professor of Law at the University of South Africa, South Africa. Before entering academic life, she practised as an attorney specializing in civil litigation. She has been admitted as attorney of the then Supreme Court of South Africa, Transvaal High Division, and of the High Court of Lesotho. She is also a qualified Trade Mark Practitioner. Kelbrick is the author of various books and articles on South African civil procedure and intellectual property enforcement.

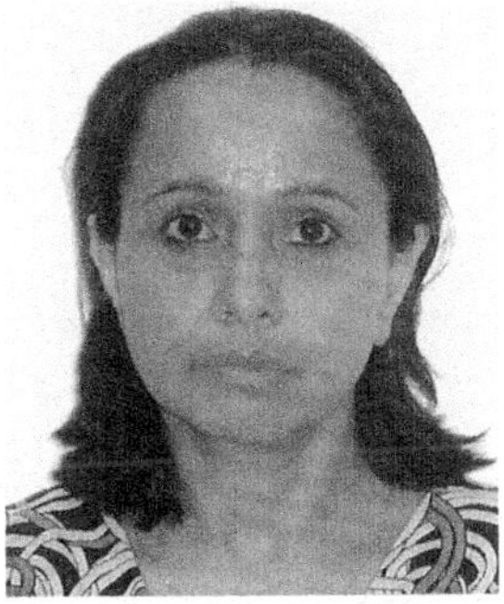

Fawzia Cassim is a former Associate Professor of Law and subject head of the civil procedure unit at the University of South Africa, South Africa. She is presently a Research Fellow in the Department of Criminal and Procedural Law at the University of South Africa, South Africa. Before entering academic life, she practised as an attorney specializing in civil and criminal litigation. She has been admitted as an attorney of the then Supreme Court of South Africa, Natal High Division and as a conveyancer of the then Supreme Court of South Africa, Transvaal High Division. She is presently practising part-time as a conveyancer in Johannesburg, South Africa.

The Authors

Dr Cassim is the author of various articles on South African civil procedure, South African criminal procedure, and cyber law.

Table of Contents

Table of Contents

Table of Contents

Table of Contents

General Introduction

Chapter 1. General Background

§1. The Political System

1. The apartheid system, in force in South Africa to a greater or lesser extent from the early days of colonial rule to April 1994, has been extensively documented and will not be described here. The first democratic multiparty elections were held during the period 26–28 April 1994. The Constitution of the Republic of South Africa 1996, referred to in this work as the Constitution, came into effect on 8 May 1996. The elections and the constitutional reforms heralded a new political age for South Africa. The African National Congress has secured the majority of votes in all subsequent elections.

2. The Constitution provides for national legislative power to be vested in the National Assembly and for some provincial legislative powers to be vested in the National Council of Provinces. Members of the National Assembly are elected by universal adult suffrage under a system of proportional representation. Parliamentary decisions are reached by a simple majority, except for constitutional amendments, which require a two-thirds majority.

3. The president is elected by the National Assembly from its members and exercises executive power together with other members of his or her cabinet. The president allocates cabinet portfolios, and cabinet decisions are reached by consensus. The first President of the democratic South Africa was Nelson Mandela. Thabo Mbeki was the second President while Jacob Zuma was the third President. Cyril Ramaphosa was officially sworn in as the new President of South Africa on 15 February 2018, following the resignation of Jacob Zuma.

4. The Constitution guarantees the powers of provincial government and recognizes the right to regional autonomy. The nine provinces each has a legislature elected under a system of proportional representation. A Constitution for each province may be drafted by its legislature, subject to the provisions of the national Constitution. The legislature elects a Premier, who heads the provincial cabinet. Provincial legislatures have primary responsibility for certain areas of government and joint powers with national government in administrative areas.

5. The judicial authority vests in the Constitutional Court, the Supreme Court of Appeal, and the High Court, which are independent of the executive authority. The structures and powers of these courts are discussed in paragraphs 35–38.

§2. The Legal System

6. South African law is not codified, and legal principles are obtained from various sources, the most important of which are legislation and judicial decisions. Contemporary South African law is derived from Roman, Dutch, and English legal systems. It has its origin in Roman law. In the Netherlands, during the fifteenth and sixteenth centuries, Roman law was adapted and combined with the customary Germanic law of the time. When the Dutch first colonized South Africa in 1652, this legal system was brought to the country and applied here. Despite subsequent British colonization, the English legal system was never adopted to replace Roman-Dutch law in South Africa. English influence on further legal development has nevertheless been profound, as portions of English law were applied piecemeal, particularly in the fields of mercantile law and civil procedure.

Chapter 2. Delimitation of the Subject Matter

§1. Definition of the Term 'Civil Procedure'

7. South African national law is divided into two primary categories, substantive law and adjective law. Substantive law defines legal rights, duties and remedies, while adjective law deals with their proof and enforcement. The manner in which legal rights are proved is dealt with in the law of evidence, while the manner in which they are enforced in civil proceedings is dealt with in that branch of adjective law known as 'civil procedure'. In South Africa, civil procedure includes proceedings in all the courts referred to in paragraph 5 above, and in all lower courts. Constitutional proceedings are also included as such proceedings can occur between persons or instances in their individual capacity.

8. Civil procedure in South Africa, as elsewhere, is criticized by various instances as restricting access to justice to the very wealthy, who can afford legal expenses, or the impoverished, who qualify for limited legal aid. Even prior to the adoption of the Constitution, attempts had been made to facilitate access to the courts and to simplify procedures. Examples of these attempts are the introduction of Small Claims Courts and the amendment of certain procedural requirements. However, it is correct that the existing procedures available to litigants can be both time-consuming and expensive.

§2. Distinction with Other Types of Procedure

9. Administrative procedure regulates the relationship between administrative bodies or organizations *inter partes* or between such bodies and persons in subordinate positions. As a general rule, when an administrative dispute arises, internally created remedies must be exhausted before a court of law may be approached for assistance. A court will usually be approached in two instances: first, when no internal remedy exists and litigation is the only remedy available to the aggrieved party, and second, when an administrative decision is subject to judicial review. In both these instances, the usual rules governing civil procedure are applied, and litigation takes place in the civil court vested with jurisdiction.

10. The rules regulating criminal procedure are completely distinct from those relating to civil procedure and are governed by separate legislation. Both civil and criminal proceedings are heard by the Constitutional Court, the High Court, and the Magistrates' Courts. Criminal proceedings may not be instituted in Small Claims Courts.

Chapter 3. Sources of Civil Procedure Law

§1. Superior Courts

11. Three sources of law can be identified in Superior Courts: (1) statute law and rules of court, (2) common law, and (3) rules of practice that have developed in different divisions of the High Court.

12. The Constitutional Court was created by the 1993 Constitution, and its powers redefined by the 1996 Constitution. The first substantive rules appeared in January 1995, while the current rules appeared in 2003. It appears that common law can be viewed as a source of procedural law in the Constitutional Court, as the Constitution provides that all Superior Courts have the inherent power to protect and regulate their own process and to develop the common law. The rules of this court also provide that the court may give such directions in matters of practice and procedure as it may consider just and expedient,[1] and no doubt High Court practice will be taken into account when giving directions, although this does not necessarily imply any inherent jurisdiction to refer to common law when legislation does not deal with a matter.

13. The Superior Courts Act 10 of 2013 consolidates and amends the laws relating to the various Superior Courts, which comprise the Constitutional Court, the Supreme Court of Appeal, and the High Court. The Act makes provision for the administration of the judicial functions of these courts, and for administrative and budgetary matters relating to them. The Chief Justice has the power to make rules for the Constitutional Court, while the Rules Board for Courts of Law has the competence to make rules for the Supreme Court of Appeal, the High Court, and all lower courts; previously, the Chief Justice and the judge-presidents of the various divisions exercised this function. The Act and the Uniform Rules do not deal fully with all procedural aspects and where these sources are silent, the inherent jurisdiction of the court to regulate its procedure permits the court to refer to common law for assistance. Because large parts of the rules are based on English practice, guidance is also sought from English decisions when dealing with aspects of procedure derived from English law, such as summary judgment, third-party procedure, and the exchange of pleadings. The Uniform Rules also create a number of discretionary powers, and practice rules have developed in the various courts aimed at achieving uniformity in the courts or at facilitating court procedure.

§2. Lower Courts

14. Lower courts are 'creatures of statute' created by legislation and deriving their powers from their enabling Act. They possess no inherent jurisdiction and may exercise only those powers expressly assigned or implied to be necessary to implement

1. Constitutional Court Rule 32(2).

legislative provisions. Rules governing their proceedings may be promulgated in terms of their enabling acts. The current rules for Magistrates' Courts appeared in 2010, and have aligned their procedure more closely to that of the High Court.

Chapter 4. General Features of the Administration of Justice in Civil Matters

§1. Characteristics of the Procedure

I. Adversary Procedure

15. The Anglo-American system of adversarial litigation is followed in all South African courts other than Small Claims Courts. This system views litigation as a private affair that a litigant may prosecute or defend without judicial interference. Trial procedure is characterized by three features: (1) the parties are responsible for the presentation of evidence in support of their submissions; (2) the judicial officer is expected to play a passive role; and (3) oral presentation of evidence and the cross-examination of parties and witnesses are emphasized. Non-trial procedures, which do not conclude with the presentation of oral evidence, are only permissible if there are no factual disputes requiring oral evidence and cross-examination.

16. Small Claims Courts represent the first move away from the adversarial system in South Africa. Here, procedural simplicity is emphasized and, apart from the document that must commence action and the response the defendant may elect to submit in writing, the judicial officer actively obtains the facts by oral questioning of both parties. The inquisitorial model is followed, and the judicial officer determines the evidence he or she wishes to hear to reach a decision. It seems likely that this is merely the first move toward a more flexible procedural system. The rules of the Constitutional Court, also reflect a less strictly adversarial approach, with the court playing a greater role in the determination of procedure and the use of applications rather than trial procedures.

II. Role of the Judge and the Parties

17. In the South African system of adversarial litigation, the role of the judicial officer is passive. The judicial officer is restricted to the evidence the parties elect to place before him or her and cannot usually augment this evidence. He or she is thus expected to reach a decision on the material placed before him or her but bears no responsibility for ensuring that this material is complete.

The role of the parties is to define the extent of the dispute and select the evidence that is presented to the court. They select the aspects of substantive law on which they wish to base their claim or defence and the procedural strategies they wish to utilize. They are responsible for conducting pretrial proceedings, collating information for presentation in evidence, summoning witnesses and presenting their cases at the trial.

They may also elect whether to prosecute a claim, raise a defence or withdraw after proceedings have commenced.

III. Written and Oral Procedure

18. In the traditionally adversarial procedure followed in the High Court and in Magistrates' Courts, proceedings always commence with the exchange of written pleadings or documents intended to formulate and define the issues between the parties. If a material dispute of fact exists, this is followed by the presentation of oral evidence, which is tested by cross-examination. If no such dispute of fact exists, no oral evidence is presented and, other than legal argument, all proceedings are written.

19. In the Constitutional Court, the procedure is written and it is for the court to decide whether it wishes to hear oral argument. In Small Claims Courts, other than the document commencing proceedings, the procedure is informal and oral.

§2. Fundamental Guarantees

I. Overview

20. Prior to the adoption of the Constitution, the fundamental guarantees afforded to litigants were not expressly stated in any formal document, but were to be found partially in legislation and partially in the unwritten element of the Westminster-model constitutional system in force in South Africa. These guarantees are now contained in the Bill of Rights in the Constitution and in legislation not in conflict with the provisions of the Constitution. The Constitution also provides that when the Bill of Rights, which deals with fundamental rights, is interpreted, the courts should have regard to international law and foreign law.[2] International human rights law must thus, for the first time, be considered when determining the fundamental guarantees afforded to litigants, as some of these guarantees are contained in the Bill of Rights. The two rights contained in this chapter that deal most specifically with litigants are the right to equality before the law and to equal protection of the law and the right to have disputes settled by a court or, where appropriate, another independent and impartial forum.[3]

21. Before the adoption of the Constitution, treaties per se did not play a large role in South African law. The president negotiated and signed international treaties, but they required statutory incorporation before having municipal application. The corresponding statute, rather than the original treaty, was the source of law. Although the president's role has remained unchanged, the Constitution now provides that Parliament decides on the ratification or accession to treaties and, once Parliament has agreed to ratification, the treaty has immediate municipal application.[4] The Constitution provides that the National Executive (which comprises the president and cabinet) is

2. Section 39(1) Constitution of the Republic of South Africa 1996.
3. Sections 9 and 34 Constitution of the Republic of South Africa 1996.
4. Section 231(1)–(5) Constitution of the Republic of South Africa 1996.

responsible for negotiating and signing all international agreements. However, such agreements only bind the Republic once approved by the National Assembly and the National Council of Provinces, unless they are of a technical, administrative or executive nature or do not require ratification or accession. An international agreement only has municipal application once enacted into law by national legislation, unless it is a self-executing provision that has been approved by Parliament. Before the adoption of the Constitution, international agreements did not play a large role in South African law, but it appears that in future, far more treaties will form part of South African law, and human rights treaties will possibly become relevant when considering fundamental guarantees.

II. Establishment of Courts by Law

22. The Constitution provides that the judicial authority of the Republic vests in the courts established by the Constitution or an Act of Parliament, and it enumerates the various courts. Section 167 describes the jurisdiction and composition of the Constitutional Court. Section 168 describes the composition and function of the Supreme Court of Appeal, while section 169 deals with the jurisdiction of the High Court. The Constitution finally provides that the establishment, jurisdiction, composition, and functioning of all other courts shall be as prescribed by or under any law.[5]

III. Independence and Impartiality

23. The Constitution provides that the judiciary shall be independent and subject only to the Constitution and the law. It also provides that no person and no organ of State shall interfere with the functioning of the court.[6] Various statutes creating the courts all provide for the presiding judicial officers of each court to take an oath of office to administer justice to all persons alike without fear, favour or prejudice. The terms of appointment of judicial officers favour independence; judges, other than Constitutional Court judges, are appointed for life, and their salaries may not be reduced while in office. Although judicial officers are paid by the state, they are not public servants. Sanctions also exist should a judicial officer not act impartially. Review proceedings may be brought against such officers presiding in lower courts, and while this procedure is not available in Superior Courts, complaint procedures do exist.

5. Section 166 Constitution of the Republic of South Africa 1996. The statutes that create courts other than the Constitutional Court, the Supreme Court of Appeal, the High Court, and the Magistrates' Courts will not be enumerated here as they are discussed when the composition of these courts is dealt with in Part I.
6. Section 165(1)–(2) Constitution of the Republic of South Africa 1996.

IV. Reasons

24. Unlike the position in regard to criminal proceedings, where legislation pertinently provides for reasons to be given for any decision which a court reaches,[7] no such provision exists for civil proceedings or civil appeals in either the Constitution or the Superior Courts Act. However, because the precedent system applies in South African law, judgments, and appeals are in the normal course accompanied by reasons. So the right of a litigant to be afforded reasons for any decision cannot be viewed as a fundamental guarantee in South African law, although it is a rule of practice that judges are expected to give reasons for their judgments. One writer advances as explanation for this practice rule the argument that an appeal on the merits would otherwise be impossible.[8] The various rules dealing with appeal procedure all presuppose the furnishing of reasons for any judgment a court makes. The procedure when noting appeal against the decision of a single judge provides that leave to appeal may be requested within fifteen days of the date of the order, but provides further that when the reasons or full reasons for the court's order are given on a later date, leave need only be requested within fifteen days of that later date.[9] Even when reasons for judgment are not given, a litigant before a single judge in the High Court and before a Magistrate is always able to request that reasons for any final judgment be furnished. In the High Court, the court may declare that reasons will be furnished to any of the parties on application,[10] while in the Magistrates' Courts any party may, after judgment, request the judicial officer to furnish a written judgment showing the facts he or she found proved and his or her reasons for judgment.[11]

V. Publicity

25. In the Cape Colony, prior to 1813, evidence and argument were heard *in camera* and only judgments and orders had to be pronounced in open court, in accordance with the then universal practice in Holland. A proclamation of 1813 required all judicial proceedings to be conducted with open doors as a matter of 'essential utility, as well as the dignity of the administration of justice'. The other colonies and provinces followed suit and, when the Supreme Court Act was promulgated in 1959, the requirement that High Court proceedings be conducted in open court, except where the court directed otherwise in special cases, applied uniformly throughout South Africa.[12] The concept 'special case' is strictly interpreted: it has been held that the emphasis should

---

7. Section 177 Criminal Procedure Act 51 of 1977: 'The court may at criminal proceedings defer its reasons for any decision on any question raised at such proceedings, and the reasons so deferred shall, when given, be deemed to have been given at the time of the proceedings.'
8. H.R. Hahlo & E. Kahn, *The South African Legal System and Its Background* 262, n. 98 (Juta 1968).
9. Uniform Rule 49(1)(b).
10. Uniform Rule 49(1)(c).
11. Magistrates' Courts Rule 51(1).
12. Section 32 Superior Courts Act 10 of 2013, *see Financial Mail (Pty) Ltd v. Registrar of Insurance* 1966(2) SA 219 (W), at 220–221 for the history of open civil courts in South Africa.

not fall on the right of the public to know or on the right of the private individual not to be embarrassed, but on the proper administration of justice.[13]

26. Neither the Constitution nor the rules of the Constitutional Court provide that proceedings of this court must take place in open court, but it is generally accepted that this is the position.

27. Provisions regarding publicity in Magistrates' Courts and Small Claims Courts are more limited. In Magistrates' Courts, the court may order *in camera* trials in the interests of good order or public morals or may direct that females or minors or the general public be denied access,[14] while in Small Claims Courts, the court may – in the interest of the administration of justice, good order or public morals or at the request of the parties for sufficient reasons – order that the proceedings be held *in camera* or that specified persons not be present.[15]

28. Various other statutes provide for proceedings to be conducted *in camera.* The Maintenance Act 99 of 1998 provides that no person whose attendance is not necessary may attend an investigation held by a maintenance court without the court's permission, while section 56 of the Children's Act 38 of 2005 provides that no person may be present at a sitting of the children's court unless his or her presence is necessary for the purpose of the proceedings.

29. Legal proceedings may be reported, provided that reports are fair and accurate. However, comments calculated to prejudice a case which is *sub judice* may not be made. The identity of witnesses or parties under the age of 18 years may not be revealed, and information disclosed during divorce proceedings may not be published.[16]

VI. Fair Trial

30. The Constitution states as a fundamental right the right to equality before the law and to equal protection and benefit of the law.[17] In addition, at common law, the maxim *audi alteram partem* has always been viewed as a cornerstone of our legal system; in the context of a fair trial, this presupposes the right of each party to be afforded an adequate opportunity to state his or her own case, which includes the right to present evidence and the right to answer his or her opponent's case. Where a party's right to the above is limited by legislation – for example, in applications for provisional sentence or summary judgment – and when ex parte applications are brought, the relevant legislation usually contains safeguards that the courts apply strictly.

13. *Cerebos Food Corporation Ltd v. Diverse Foods Sa (Pty) Ltd* 1984(4) SA 149 (T), at 158.
14. Section 5 Magistrates' Courts Act 32 of 1944.
15. Section 4(1)–(2) Small Claims Courts Act 61 of 1984.
16. Section 12 Divorce Act 70 of 1979.
17. Section 9(1) Constitution of the Republic of South Africa 1996.

VII. Reasonable Time

31. To enjoy equal protection of the law, each party requires adequate notice of proceedings and adequate time to prepare his or her case. Adequate notice necessitates the issue of a summons or notice of motion setting out the relief claimed and additionally informing the other party of the institution of proceedings by service of this process. Detailed requirements for the ways in which service can be effected are contained in the rules regulating all South African courts, and proceedings cannot continue until defence has been entered or the time for entry has elapsed. In addition, if default judgment has been obtained because the defendant did not receive notice, it may be set aside.

32. To prepare his or her case, a party also requires sufficient information of his or her opponent's case timeously, to avoid being taken by surprise at the hearing of the matter. This right finds expression in the exchange of pleadings, the rules that set out the information to be contained in a pleading and the various discovery mechanisms.

VIII. Appeal

33. There is no general right to appeal against the judgment of a court. Appeal from any decision of a Superior Court may only be noted with the consent of the court that gave the judgment or the court to which the appeal is directed. No appeal lies from the decision of a Small Claims Court, although the proceedings can be taken on review in specific circumstances. The only right to appeal exists from decisions of Magistrates' Courts, where a party may appeal to the appropriate High Court.

Part I. Judicial Organization

Chapter 1. The Courts and Their Members

§1. Courts

I. Structure of the Court System

34. Historically, the Republic of South Africa comprised a union of four Southern African British colonies. These four colonies, the Cape Colony, Orange River Colony, Natal, and Transvaal, surrendered their sovereign rights and became the Union of South Africa on 31 May 1910. Prior to unification, each colony had its own Superior Court. Even today this is reflected in the South African court structure. The basic division of South African courts is into Superior Courts, which have inherent jurisdiction, and lower courts, which have no inherent jurisdiction and whose duties and powers are statutorily prescribed.

A. Superior Courts

35. The primary distinction here is between the Constitutional Court, the Supreme Court of Appeal, and the High Court.[18] The Constitutional Court has jurisdiction, either as original court or as Court of Final Instance, over all matters relating to the interpretation, protection and enforcement of the Constitution, and over non-constitutional matters that the court considers raise an arguable point of law of general public importance.[19] The Supreme Court of Appeal has no original jurisdiction and hears only appeals from the High Court, except for labour and competition matters.[20] A litigant may therefore not approach this court directly but only after a decision has already been made by another Superior Court.

36. Various divisions of the High Court exist, which correspond to the nine different provinces of South Africa. These divisions have original jurisdiction over

18. Prior to the 1996 Constitution, the Supreme Court of Appeal was known as the Appellate Division of the Supreme Court, while the various High Courts were known as (named) Provincial or Local Divisions of the Supreme Court.
19. Section 167(3)–(7) Constitution of the Republic of South Africa 1996.
20. Section 168(3) Constitution of the Republic of South Africa 1996.

their territorial area. In addition, more local seats for a division may be created to serve heavily populated areas of the country. The main seat of a division has concurrent appeal jurisdiction over the area of any local seats.

37. A High Court is empowered to hear appeals from lower courts in its area and full bench appeals from judgments made by single judges in their respective courts and courts over which they exercise concurrent jurisdiction.

38. The Judge-President of a High Court may, by notice in the Government Gazette, divide the area of jurisdiction into circuit districts. In each such district a court known as a local Circuit Court is held at least twice a year. This court is presided over by a judge of the relevant High Court.[21]

39. Various specialist Superior Courts also exist. Special courts exist to hear income tax appeals and appeals against the assessment of estate duty.[22] The President of such a court is a judge of the High Court, who sits together with a senior accountant and a member of the commercial community. Appeals against questions of law (as opposed to questions of fact) are allowed to a High Court. The Labour Court is a Superior Court with exclusive jurisdiction in respect of various matters relating to labour issues and concurrent jurisdiction with the High Court in respect of infringements of fundamental rights arising from employment or labour relations.[23]

40. Intellectual property matters are also in certain instances heard by specialist courts. For patents, the Judge-President of the Gauteng Division designates a judge of that court to act as commissioner of patents. The commissioner has jurisdiction in the first instance to decide proceedings relating to patents and has the powers and jurisdiction of a single judge in civil proceedings when doing so.[24] Appeals from his or her decision lie to a full bench of this division. In trademark cases, although the registrar of trademarks is not a judge, certain orders made by him or her have the same status as those made by a single judge.[25] Appeals from his or her decision lie to a full bench of the Gauteng Division. The commissioner of patents is also the copyright tribunal and as such determines disputes concerning copyright licences.[26] An appeal from his or her decision also lies to a full bench.

41. The Competition Appeal Court exists to hear appeals from persons who are affected by a decision of the Competition Tribunal on contraventions of the Competition Act.[27] The court is constituted by the president and consists of at least three High Court judges. No appeal or review lies from a decision of this court. The Constitution provides for the restitution of rights in land in respect of persons or communities who were dispossessed under racially discriminatory laws, and a Land Claims Court has been created to hear such matters. This court has countrywide jurisdiction to determine restitution of land rights and compensation claims and to determine persons entitled

21. Section 7 Superior Courts Act 10 of 2013.
22. Sections 116–118 Tax Administration Act 28 of 2011 and s. 24 Estate Duty Act 45 of 1955.
23. Section 157 Labour Relations Act 66 of 1995; *see also* s. 168(3)(a) Constitution of the Republic of South Africa 1996.
24. Sections 8, 17 and 18 Patents Act 57 of 1978.
25. Sections 45(1) and 53 Trade Marks Act 194 of 1993.
26. Section 29 Copyright Act 98 of 1978.
27. Sections 36(1), 62 of the Competition Act 89 of 1998; *see also* s. 168(3)(a) Constitution of the Republic of South Africa 1996.

to ownership. The court is constituted by the president and consists of a president and additional judges.[28]

B. Lower Courts

42. Lower courts are created by statute. The jurisdiction of these courts is limited as regards the type of action that may be heard, the amount claimed, and the persons concerned. The country is divided into districts and a Magistrate's Court exists for every district. Magistrates' Courts hear civil claims for lower amounts than those heard by the High Court. An appeal of right lies from a decision of a Magistrates' Court to the relevant High Court. Small civil claims are heard by Small Claims Courts, which exist for areas equivalent to magisterial districts.

43. Other specialist courts cannot be classified as either superior or lower courts. Not all such courts will be mentioned here. Children's courts exist to deal with adoption matters, contribution orders, investigations concerning children in need of care and temporary custody.[29] Every Magistrate's Court is also a children's court for its area of jurisdiction. Military courts have jurisdiction over members of the defence force for offences under the Defence Act or under the military discipline code.[30]

C. The Precedent System (Stare Decisis)

44. The term *stare decisis* means 'to stand by decisions'. In South Africa, this doctrine is applied in the following way: when a decision on a legal principle has been given by a Superior Court, it should be followed by all courts of equal or lower status. The structure of the courts, set out above, determines the implementation of this doctrine. One of the reasons for the application of the precedent system in South Africa is that the law is not set out in a general code, unlike civil law systems. The doctrine, although criticized as leading to rigidity and lack of legal development, is expedient. It avoids uncertainty, protects established rights and prevents unnecessary litigation. The whole judgment does not bind other courts but only that portion termed the *ratio decidendi* (i.e., the legal principle on which the court bases its decision). Decisions on questions of fact are not binding. Obiter dicta, which are expressions of opinion pronounced incidentally by the court, are also not binding but have strong persuasive value.

45. The doctrine is applied as follows in South African courts: a decision of the Constitutional Court binds all other courts. The Supreme Court of Appeal is bound by all its previous decisions, unless it is convinced that a previous judgment was incorrect. All previous decisions are equally binding, irrespective of how many judges concurred in the decision. All other superior and lower courts are bound by decisions of the Supreme Court of Appeal, even if incorrect. A decision given by more than one judge (a full bench) is binding on other Superior Courts in the same territorial area comprising an equal number or fewer judges. A full bench is not bound by the decision of a single

28. Section 25 Constitution of the Republic of South Africa 1996; ss 22–38 Restitution of Land Rights Act 22 of 1994.
29. Section 42 Children's Act 38 of 2005.
30. Section 6 Military Discipline Supplementary Measures Act 16 of 1999.

judge in the same division. However, between divisions of the High Court in different provinces, the doctrine is not enforced, and a bench in one division may reach a decision differing from that reached by a bench comprising an equal number of judges in a division in another province. Magistrates' Courts are bound by the judgments of all Superior Courts. If a conflict exists between such courts, a Magistrate must follow the decision of his or her own division of the High Court. Magistrates are not bound by the decisions of other Magistrates, in part because such decisions are not reported.

II. Administration of the Court

A. Superior Courts

46. The Constitutional Court, the Supreme Court of Appeal, and the divisions of the High Court all have their seat in a determined place specified by statute. As many courts may sit at a particular time as the available judges allow. Each Superior Court may make rules regulating the times at which it will sit.[31] Usually, each court has four terms per year, and only urgent matters will be heard during recess periods. The Chief Administrative Officer of each court is known as a registrar. His or her office oversees the running of that court, including the issue, receipt and storage of court process, and the enrolment of cases for hearing by the court. Superior Courts are courts of record, and the public has access to court records. Unless exceptional circumstances exist, all proceedings must take place in open court. Parties and witnesses may, during proceedings, use the South African language of their choice.[32] Provision is made for the translation of records or other documents filed at the Constitutional Court, which are written in an official language not understood by all the judges.[33]

B. Lower Courts

47. Magistrates' Courts are constituted for specific districts, and each court is situated in a specified place within that district. As many courts may sit at the same time in each district as the number of Magistrates permits. Magistrates' Courts sit throughout the year. The Administrative Officer in a Magistrate's Court is known as the clerk of the court. All defended civil trials must take place in open court, unless the presiding Magistrate directs otherwise. Proceedings may take place in any official language. Records are kept of all proceedings, and the public has access to these records.[34]

48. The area of Small Claims Courts and their seats usually correspond to the magisterial district within which they fall. Although such courts sit throughout the year, hearings usually take place after working hours due to the fact that the commissioners of such courts are frequently attorneys or advocates in private practice. The clerk of the court is responsible for its administration. Proceedings are conducted in open court

31. Rule 2 Constitutional Court Rules; s. 51 Superior Courts Act 10 of 2013; Uniform Rule 2.
32. Section 30 Constitution of the Republic of South Africa, 1996.
33. Rule 25 Constitutional Court Rules.
34. Section 7 Magistrates' Courts Act 32 of 1944.

unless exceptional circumstances exist. These courts are not courts of record, and only the judgment is recorded. Proceedings may take place in any official language but, if evidence is given in any language with which one of the parties is not conversant, the court will provide an interpreter.

III. Bench

A. Superior Courts

49. The Constitutional Court consists of the Chief Justice of South Africa, a Deputy Chief Justice, and nine other judges who serve for a non-renewable term of twelve years.[35]

The Supreme Court of Appeal[36] consists of a president, a deputy president, and a number of judges of appeal. A quorum of five judges is required when civil appeals are heard. The judgment of the majority of judges is the judgment of the court. If it appears to the Chief Justice that in view of the importance of a matter under appeal, it should be heard by a larger number of judges than usually provided, he or she may make directions to this effect; if the hearing has already commenced, he or she may discontinue it and direct that it be commenced anew before as many judges as he or she considers necessary. If a judge becomes incapable of acting during the hearing of an appeal through death, retirement or some other reason, the hearing of the appeal may continue before the remainder of the judges concerned, and the judgment of the majority of the remainder becomes the judgment of the court. A judge may not sit at the hearing of an appeal against a judgment given in a case which was heard before him or her.

50. Each division of the High Court consists of a judge-president, a deputy judge-president, and various judges.

51. A High Court sitting as Court of First Instance (i.e., a matter coming before a court for the first time) is constituted before a single judge of that division. Provision has been made that the judge-president may direct that such a matter be heard by more judges, although in practice this rarely happens. A single judge may also, during a hearing, discontinue a matter and refer it to a court composed of more judges. Where an appeal is heard from a lower court, it must be heard by at least two judges. Appeals against judgments of a single Judge of a High Court must be heard by three judges. No judge may sit at the hearing of an appeal against a judgment given in a case which was heard before him or her. Where more than one judge is sitting at a hearing, the judgment of the majority is the judgment of the court. Where a majority cannot be obtained, hearings are commenced de novo before a new court constituted at the judge-president's determination. If one of the presiding judges dies or retires, or becomes otherwise incapable of acting during a full court hearing, the hearing proceeds before the remaining judges if they constitute a majority of the judges before whom it was commenced. If the remaining judges do not constitute a majority, or if only one

35. Section 176(1) Constitution of the Republic of South Africa 1996.

36. *See* ss 5, 13, 14 Superior Courts Act 10 of 2013.

judge remains, the hearing is commenced de novo, unless all the parties concerned agree in writing to accept the decision of the remaining judge or judges.

52. The Superior Courts Act[37] also provides for the appointment of referees during civil proceedings in certain limited instances. A court may, with the consent of the parties concerned, refer matters for enquiry and report to a referee and may then deal with the report as it deems fit. The matters that may be referred are those which require extensive examination of documents or scientific, technical or local investigation that the court feels it cannot conveniently conduct or matters that relate to accounts. Any report or part thereof which is adopted by the court has the force of a finding of the court concerned. For the purpose of an enquiry, a referee has the powers and must conduct the enquiry as prescribed by the court concerned or by the rules of court.

53. The judicial officers mentioned above are the only persons who may preside in a Superior Court when court proceedings are heard. No provision is made in South African civil proceedings for juries, assessors or the like.

B. Lower Courts

54. In lower courts, only one judicial officer presides during the hearing of a civil matter. No provision exists for juries, assessors or the like.

§2. Members of the Judiciary

I. Superior Courts

55. All Constitutional and High Court judges are appointed by the President of the Republic on the advice of the Judicial Services Commission. This commission comprises the Minister of Justice, the Chief Justice, the President of the Supreme Court of Appeal, one Judge-President of a High Court, various legal practitioners and academics, and some nominated members of national and provincial government. The function of the commission is to advise the national and provincial governments on matters relating to the judiciary and the administration of justice and to make recommendations regarding the appointment and removal of judges. When making judicial appointments, the need for the judiciary to reflect broadly the racial and gender composition of South Africa must be considered.[38]

Constitutional Court:[39] judges of the Constitutional Court must all be South African citizens and be fit and proper persons. The Constitutional Court is headed by the Chief Justice of South Africa, who is appointed after consultation with the Judicial Services Commission and the leaders of parties represented in the National Assembly. Other judges of the Constitutional Court are also appointed by the president from lists of nominees compiled by the Judicial Services Commission. There are eleven judges of the Constitutional Court, of whom at least four must be persons who were judges

37. Section 38 Superior Courts Act 10 of 2013.
38. Sections 174, 177 and 178 Constitution of the Republic of South Africa 1996.
39. Sections 167(1) and 174 Constitution of the Republic of South Africa 1996.

at the time they were appointed to the Constitutional Court. A constitutional judge may resign from office by notice in writing to the President of the Republic.[40]

56. High Court:[41] all judges of the High Court must be fit and proper persons and are appointed by the President of the Republic acting on the advice of the Judicial Services Commission. The statutory requirement that the person must be 'fit and proper' implies that anyone, whether or not he or she has legal training, may be appointed as judge. In practice, appointments are made from senior counsel at the bar or other persons involved in the practice or teaching of law. Judges of the High Court who held office immediately before the commencement of the Constitution are deemed to have been duly appointed to the corresponding positions in terms of the Constitution. The number of High Court judges who may be appointed is not limited, and the president may appoint as many judges as necessary to deal with the volume of work. Apart from permanent appointments, the Minister of Justice can also appoint acting judges to a specific court for a particular period. Such acting judges are usually senior counsel of the bar or senior attorneys who return to their practices after their period of appointment has expired.

57. Remuneration: the salaries, allowances, and benefits of all judges are prescribed by legislation and paid by the State from revenue and may not be reduced.[42] No judge may hold any other office of profit or receive remuneration for any other service without the consent of the Minister of Justice.

II. End of Functions and Discipline

58. Constitutional Court judges are appointed for a non-renewable twelve-year period.[43] They must serve a total of fifteen years as judge, unless they reach the age of 75 before expiry of this total period. High Court judges must retire from active service when they reach the age of 70 years, provided they have completed a period of active service of at least ten years. This is subject to a provision that permits certain judges to serve up to the age of 75 years, or until a service period of fifteen years has been completed, whichever occurs sooner. If they have not completed this period of service, they are discharged immediately on completion thereof. A judge who has reached the age of 65 years and performed active service for fifteen years may resign from office by notice in writing to the president. A judge may only be removed from office by the President of the Republic on the grounds of incapacity, gross incompetence or gross misconduct if so found by the Judicial Services Commission and upon receipt of a resolution from the National Assembly calling for such removal. A judge who is the subject of such an investigation by the commission may be suspended by the president pending its outcome. A judge may also be discharged by the president if he or she becomes inflicted with a permanent infirmity of mind or body and may, at his

40. Section 11 Judges' Remuneration and Conditions of Employment Act 47 of 2001.
41. *See* ss 174(6), 175(2) and Sch. 6 s. 16 Constitution of the Republic of South Africa 1996; s. 6 Superior Courts Act 10 of 2013.
42. Section 176(3) Constitution of the Republic of South Africa 1996.
43. Section 176(1), 177 Constitution of the Republic of South Africa 1996; ss 3–4 Judges' Remuneration and Conditions of Employment Act 47 of 2001.

or her own request, be discharged from service if there is a reason the president deems sufficient. In all instances, on discharge from active service a judge receives a tax-free gratuity and continues to receive a salary until his or her death.

III. Judicial Officers in Lower Courts

A. Magistrates' Courts

59. A Magistrates' Commission was created in terms of the 1993 Constitution to ensure that the appointment, promotion, transfer or dismissal of, or disciplinary steps against Magistrates, take place without favour or prejudice; that the applicable laws and administrative directives in this regard are applied uniformly and properly; and that no victimization or improper influencing of Magistrates occurs.[44] The Minister of Justice or his or her delegate appoints Magistrates subject to the recommendations of this commission. The Magistrates who preside in Magistrates' Courts are appointed in a full-time capacity. Minimum qualifications are prescribed for appointment as a Magistrate. The minister may appoint as many Magistrates as necessary for the orderly functioning of Magistrates' Courts. He or she may also appoint acting Magistrates whenever a Magistrate is by reason of absence or incapacity unable to carry out his or her office, for the period of such vacancy. Such acting Magistrates need not comply with the minimum requirements set out above. Magistrates may be suspended or removed from office for misconduct, ill health or incapacity to carry out their duties of office efficiently.

B. Other Courts

60. The presiding officer in a Small Claims Court is known as a commissioner.[45] Commissioners are appointed by the Minister of Justice, who may delegate this authority to a Magistrate of the district. Commissioners are advocates, attorneys, legal academics or ex-Magistrates who have been involved in legal practice for at least seven years. They serve part-time on a rotating basis and receive no remuneration for this work. Commissioners are appointed for a three-year period but may resign at any time by notice in writing to the minister. No state employee may be appointed as commissioner. The minister may at any time withdraw the appointment of a commissioner if in his or her opinion there is sufficient reason for doing so.

44. *See* ss 4, 13, 18 Magistrates Act 90 of 1993; ss 9, 10 Magistrates' Courts Act 32 of 1944.
45. *See* s. 9 Small Claims Courts Act 61 of 1984.

Chapter 2. The Bar

§1. Exercise of the Legal Profession

61. South Africa has a divided bar, comprising advocates and attorneys. Dual practice as both advocate and attorney is not permitted. While all advocates can appear in both superior and lower courts, only attorneys in possession of a *baccalaureus legum* degree and an admission certificate may appear in Superior Courts, while other attorneys only have a right of appearance in Magistrates' Courts. However, an advocate cannot appear in a civil matter unless he or she is instructed to do so by an attorney.

62. The Legal Practice Act 28 of 2014 came into force in September 2014 but will only take effect over a number of years. The purpose of this Act is to create a single regulatory body, to ensure that legal services are accessible to the public and that entry into the profession is unrestricted, so as to bring the legal profession in line with the ideals of the Constitution. The Act will in first instance create a transitional entity called the National Forum on the Legal Profession which will make recommendations to the Minister of Justice on training requirements, and on the merging of the various existing control bodies into a single South African Legal Practice Council, which will regulate the conduct of all practitioners, both advocates and attorneys. The Legal Practice Amendment Bill was recently debated before the National Assembly. It seeks to facilitate a smooth transition from the current dispensation to new structures prescribed in the Legal Practice Act. It also stipulates a time period for the election of a new Attorneys Fidelity Fund Board. The Legal Practice Bill allows the National Forum until 31 October 2018 to fulfil its mandate and hand over control to the Legal Practice Council. The Legal Practice Bill was passed into law as the Legal Practice Amendment Act 16 of 2017. It came into operation on 18 January 2018.

As implementation of this Act will not take place in the near future, the existing position will be dealt with now.

I. Conditions for Admission

63. Advocates:[46] an advocate must comply with both general requirements and academic qualifications before he or she is admitted to practice as such. An advocate must be over the age of 21 and must satisfy the court that he or she is a fit and proper person to be admitted and enrolled. 'Fit and proper' has been held in various decisions to mean that admission of the applicant involves no danger to the public and no danger to the good name of the profession. Race, gender, and religious belief are not a consideration for admission. An advocate must also be a South African citizen or be permanently resident in South Africa and apply for citizenship within six years from the date of admission to South Africa as a permanent resident. An applicant for admission as advocate may not be an enrolled attorney. The academic qualification required for

46. The Admission of Advocates Act 74 of 1964 governs the admission and conduct of advocates.

admission is a *baccalaureus legum* degree from any university in South Africa after a study period of not less than four years, or various statutorily defined equivalents. To obtain admission as advocate, the applicant must apply ex parte to court for admission to practise and authority to be enrolled as an advocate. Notice must be given to the Bar Council and, if the court grants the order, the advocate's name will be enrolled on the roll of advocates kept by the Secretary for Justice. However, to become a member of the Bar of a High Court, an advocate must additionally serve a one-year pupillage with an existing member and thereafter successfully complete the national bar examination set by the General Council of the Bar. Advocates have the right to charge reasonable fees for their work, and the instructing attorney is liable for payment of such fees.

64. Attorneys:[47] various requirements must be met before a person will be admitted and enrolled as an attorney. He or she must be a fit and proper person, over the age of 21 and a South African citizen or a permanent resident. He or she must hold a *baccalaureus legum* degree. In addition, he or she must have served a minimum period of one year as a candidate attorney and have completed a law society approved training course or law society approved community service for a specified period. He or she must also pass the practical examinations set by the law society. If these requirements are satisfied, a court will, on application, admit and enrol the applicant as attorney. Enrolment entitles an attorney to practise within the jurisdiction of the court where he or she has been admitted. Enrolment as notary or conveyancer requires the successful completion of additional examination and prior or simultaneous admission as attorney.

II. Rights and Duties

65. Advocates: an advocate's primary duty is to uphold the interests of his or her client without misleading the court. He or she must therefore disclose all material facts of which he or she has knowledge to the court but on the contrary may not breach clients' confidences. An advocate is under a duty to accept a brief if he or she is available. Advocates must practise for their own account and may not be employed or enter into partnerships. They may not advertise or canvass for work.

66. Attorneys: certain types of work may only be done for remuneration by attorneys (e.g., the initiation of litigation, the drafting of certain documents, property transfers and the rendering of certain legal services). A practising attorney must deposit all money held on behalf of other persons in a trust account. He or she must keep proper books of account that are open to inspection by the law society. Statutory tariffs control attorneys' remuneration for various types of work (e.g., litigation, conveyancing, and notarial work). However, an attorney may agree with his or her client to charge an additional fee. Where no statutory tariff exists, an attorney may not charge excessive fees and, if a client complains, such fees may be assessed by the law society. Limited provision exists in South Africa for the payment of contingency fees (i.e., remuneration by result).

47. The Attorneys Act 53 of 1979 governs the attorneys' profession.

III. Discipline

67. An advocate will be suspended or disbarred by court if it is found that he or she is no longer a fit and proper person to continue to practise as an advocate. Such applications are usually instituted by the Bar Council to which the advocate belongs.

68. Discipline over attorneys is exercised in the first instance by the various law societies, each of which has detailed codes of conduct. In appropriate instances, a disciplinary inquiry will be held and if an attorney is found guilty of unprofessional or dishonourable conduct, the law society may fine or reprimand him or her. In more serious instances, the law society will apply to court to have the attorney suspended from practice or struck from the roll.

§2. Public Institutions and Private Organizations

I. Professional Bodies

69. The divisional structure of the High Court is reflected in the professional bodies of both advocates and attorneys. A bar, which is the controlling body for all advocates practising in that court, exists for every High Court. Each bar protects the interests of its members and supervises their conduct. Each bar has a Bar Council, chosen annually by its members, which has wide powers over its members and enforces discipline. The various bars are federated into the general council of the bar, which upholds the interests of members on a national and an international level. The various bars and the general council are not statutorily regulated, and membership of a bar is not a prerequisite for practise as an advocate. Membership is conditional on successful completion of a period of pupillage and the national bar examination.

70. A number of provincial law societies exist that are the controlling bodies for attorneys practising in that area. The law societies are statutorily regulated and membership by all practitioners is compulsory. The various law societies protect the interests of their members and control their professional conduct. The various law societies have established the Law Society of South Africa, an umbrella body that coordinates activities on a national level. Unlike the provincial law societies, this body has no statutory or disciplinary powers.

II. Public Institutions

71. The information set out above deals with legal practitioners in private practice. However, advocates and attorneys may also be employed by the State. State advocates are usually employed in the criminal prosecution of serious offences in Superior Courts. The State Attorney's Office, under the control of the Minister of Justice, performs all the work usually done by attorneys, notaries, and conveyancers on behalf of the government of South Africa. Their rights and duties are similar to those of private practitioners, and they also fall under the control of the relevant law society.

Chapter 3. The Sheriffs (Bailiffs)

72. Sheriffs are responsible for the service of court process and the execution of all court orders, including warrants, in both Superior Courts and lower courts.[48] Sheriffs are not members of the civil service, but practise for own account although their tariff of fees is regulated by statute. They are appointed by the Minister of Justice and Constitutional Development, assisted by an advisory committee. A controlling body, the Board of Sheriffs, exercises control over sheriffs and may take disciplinary steps against its members. Legislation details the disqualifications for appointment to the office of sheriff and the suspension and removal of sheriffs. In terms of the Judicial Matters Amendment Act of 2017, the Board of Sheriffs is now obliged to issue a fidelity fund certificate for a sheriff pending his or her appointment by the minister.[49]

48. The Sheriffs Act 90 of 1986 governs sheriffs.
49. Section 18 of Judicial Matters Amendment Act 8 of 2017.

Part II. Jurisdiction

Chapter 1. Domestic Jurisdiction

§1. Subject Matter Jurisdiction

73. The internal jurisdiction of South African courts is closely related to the structure of the court system. The Constitutional Court, an entity separate from the various High Courts, is the Court of Final Instance and its jurisdiction is prescribed by the Constitution. It has both original jurisdiction in respect of certain constitutional matters and appeal jurisdiction concerning constitutional matters decided by other courts, and non-constitutional matters which it considers fall within its jurisdiction. The Supreme Court of Appeal functions as a Court of Appeal in respect of both constitutional and non-constitutional matters. The High Court primarily exercises jurisdiction in terms of the common law and, other than matters excluded by the Constitution, has jurisdiction to hear any type of action. Lower courts, including Magistrates' and Small Claims Courts, have limited jurisdiction that is statutorily prescribed.

I. Constitutional Court

74. The jurisdiction of the Constitutional Court is governed by the Constitution. This court has original and exclusive jurisdiction to hear inquiries into the constitutionality of Acts of Parliament or provincial legislation, disputes over the constitutionality of parliamentary or provincial bills, disputes of a constitutional nature between organs of State at national or provincial level, and the determination of questions whether any matter falls within its jurisdiction.[50] The Constitutional Court also has appeal jurisdiction in respect of constitutional matters decided by the Supreme Court of Appeal or the High Courts, and in respect of non-constitutional matters which it considers raise an arguable point of law of general public importance.

50. Section 167(3)–(4) Constitution of the Republic of South Africa 1996.

II. Supreme Court of Appeal

75. This court has jurisdiction to hear all appeals and reviews from the High Court, except in respect of labour and competition matters as determined by an Act of Parliament. A further appeal to the Constitutional Court is possible in respect of constitutional issues and other issues which the Constitutional Court considers to be of general public importance.

III. High Courts

76. The structure of the High Court resembles that of a federation, rather than a unitary state, and each of the divisions operates to a large extent independently. Jurisdictional issues usually relate to territory – that is, which court is entitled to hear a matter – as all the courts have unlimited subject matter jurisdiction except in respect of certain constitutional matters and certain appeals.

77. The Constitution grants jurisdiction to the High Court to decide any constitutional matter except one that the Constitutional Court has agreed to hear directly, or that is assigned to another court by legislation, as well as any other matter not assigned to another court by legislation.[51]

IV. Lower Courts

78. Magistrates' and Small Claims Courts have limited subject matter jurisdiction. Magistrates' Courts may not enquire into or rule on the constitutionality of any legislation or any conduct of the president. They also do not have jurisdiction to hear matters in which the validity or interpretation of a will or testamentary document is in question, in which the status of a person in respect of mental capacity is sought to be affected, in which specific performance without an alternative claim for damages is sought – except in the rendering of an account or the delivery or transfer of movable or immovable property up to a specified financial amount – or in which a decree of perpetual silence is sought. Regional Magistrates' Courts, unlike district courts, may hear divorce and related actions.[52] Consent by the parties concerned cannot grant jurisdiction to a court which is not vested with jurisdiction.

79. Small Claims Courts may also not hear such matters and in addition do not have jurisdiction to grant interdicts or to hear matters in which damages are sought in respect of defamation, malicious prosecution, wrongful imprisonment or arrest, seduction or breach of promise to marry.[53]

80. Both courts may also not hear matters where the claim exceeds a specified sum of money. In respect of Magistrates' Courts, the current financial limit is South Africa Rand (ZAR) 200,000, although regional Magistrates' Courts may hear claims

51. Section 169 Constitution of the Republic of South Africa 1996.
52. Section 170 Constitution of the Republic of South Africa 1996; s. 29(1B), s. 46 Magistrates' Courts Act 32 of 1944.
53. Section 16 Small Claims Courts Act 61 of 1984.

of amounts between ZAR 200,000 and ZAR 400,000.[54] The financial limitation for all claims instituted in Small Claims Courts is currently ZAR 15,000. In both courts, if the sum claimed does not exceed the jurisdictional limit and is the balance of an account, the court may enquire into and hear evidence on the whole account, even though the account relates to items and transactions exceeding the court's jurisdiction. A court is also not deprived of jurisdiction merely because it is necessary, in order to arrive at a decision on a claim falling within its jurisdiction, to give a finding on a matter outside its jurisdiction. In determining whether a claim falls within the jurisdiction of the court, claims for interest, costs or general or alternative relief are not taken into account.[55] Parties may abandon part of their claim or deduct an admitted debt to bring a claim within the jurisdiction of either court. Small Claims Courts do not have jurisdiction over the State as defendant and do not have jurisdiction in respect of claims or counterclaims based on a cession or assignment of rights.[56]

§2. Venue (Territorial Jurisdiction)

81. Both the Constitutional Court and the Supreme Court of Appeal have countrywide jurisdiction. However as noted above, the structure of the divisions of the High Court resembles that of a federation, with each province being served by a court. In addition, where numbers necessitate it, further courts with a more limited geographical area of jurisdiction exist, which then have concurrent jurisdiction within their area with the relevant provincial divisions other than in respect of appeals and reviews. While the constitutional jurisdiction of the Superior Courts has been discussed under subject matter jurisdiction, the Constitution grants these courts the jurisdiction vested in them prior to its commencement and also statutorily confirms their inherent power. Inherent power is understood as the power to protect and regulate their own process and to develop the common law taking into account the interests of justice.[57]

I. High Court

82. Other than the Constitution, the primary statute regulating the jurisdiction of the High Court is the Superior Courts Act, which provides that 'A Division has jurisdiction over all persons residing or being in, and in relation to all causes arising… within its area of jurisdiction and all other matters of which it may according to law take cognisance.'[58] This does not, however, mean that the jurisdiction of this court is statutorily regulated, as numerous decisions have held that the common law determines jurisdiction by interpreting the phrase 'causes arising' as meaning 'legal proceedings duly arising, that is to say, proceedings in which the court has jurisdiction under the

54. Section 29 Magistrates' Courts Act 32 of 1944.
55. Section 37 Magistrates' Courts Act 32 of 1944; s. 17 Small Claims Courts Act 61 of 1984.
56. Section 14(2), (4) Small Claims Courts Act 61 of 1984.
57. Section 173 Constitution of the Republic of South Africa 1996.
58. Section 21 Superior Courts Act 10 f 2013.

common law'.[59] Unless legislation has intervened, it is therefore always necessary to determine the common law position to decide when a High Court is vested with jurisdiction.

83. Terminology. The common law basis of High Court jurisdiction has resulted in the use of various terms originating from Roman law. As these terms have been modified and adapted for local use, their meaning might differ from the meaning assigned elsewhere in the world. A short summary of the most frequently used terms is therefore provided. An *incola* is a person domiciled or resident within a specific court's jurisdictional area. The concept of an *incola* of the whole of South Africa does not exist. A peregrine is either a local peregrine (i.e., not domiciled or resident within that particular court's area but an *incola* of some other South African court) or a foreign peregrine (i.e., someone not domiciled or resident anywhere in South Africa). Citizenship is irrelevant when determining these concepts. Domicile is acquired by lawful presence at a particular place with the intention of settling there for an indefinite period.[60] Residence is something less than domicile but amounts to more than mere physical presence in a place. In determining residence, our courts have stated that a person can be domiciled in one place and resident in another; that a person can have more than one place of residence in which case he or she should be sued from the court where he or she is residing at the time of service of the summons. Such a person is not viewed as resident at a place which he or she visits temporarily. Some or other *ratio jurisdictionis* or jurisdictional connecting factor between a specific court and the defendant or the cause of action is always required by common law rules of jurisdiction. Factors that are accepted include domicile or residence of the defendant, commission of a delict, creation or breach of a contract, prorogation (submission or consent) in certain circumstances, and the situation of property that relates to the dispute.

84. Different jurisdictional principles are applied in the High Court, depending on the type of claim concerned. These can be categorized as money claims, property claims and claims affecting status.

85. Money claims. The term 'money claim', or claim sounding in money, refers to any claim in which the payment of money is sought as relief, whether as the principal claim or as an alternative claim. The overriding principle in respect of such claims is the 'doctrine of effectiveness'; that is, the court must be in a position to give a meaningful judgment in that it is able to exercise some control over the defendant or his or her property. Differing rules apply depending on the status of the defendant. If he or she is an *incola* of some court in South Africa, that court may always exercise jurisdiction in accordance with the Roman law maxim *actor sequitur forum rei*. Where more than one court has jurisdiction on this ground – that is, the defendant is domiciled within one court's jurisdictional area and resident in another – either court may hear the matter. In addition, any court where the cause of action arose, either wholly or in part, may exercise jurisdiction. Thus, the court where the delict was committed or where the contract was concluded or breached also has jurisdiction. The situation of the plaintiff is irrelevant and does not affect the court's exercise of jurisdiction. The defendant need also not be present within the court's jurisdictional area at the time action is instituted.

---

59. *Ewing McDonald & Co. Ltd v. M & M Products Co.* 1991 (1) SA 252 (A) at 257.
60. Section 1(2) Domicile Act 3 of 1992.

86. Where the defendant is a peregrine of the whole of South Africa, the position changes. Two possible courts might be able to exercise jurisdiction: the court of which the plaintiff is an *incola* or the court where the cause of action arose. However, in both instances the court will only be vested with jurisdiction if, in addition, attachment of the defendant's property takes place somewhere within South Africa. If the plaintiff is an *incola* of the court and attachment can be effected, such attachment founds jurisdiction where it would otherwise not have existed. If the cause of action arose within the jurisdictional area of a court and attachment can be effected, this confirms an existing partial jurisdiction. If attachment is not possible, a court may assume jurisdiction if the defendant is served with the summons while in South Africa, and there is an adequate connection between the action and the court's jurisdictional area.[61] If the defendant is not present or does not own property in South Africa, no South African court will be competent to exercise jurisdiction and litigation must be instituted elsewhere. If the defendant submits to the jurisdiction of the court, an attachment becomes unnecessary.[62]

87. Property claims. In terms of the common law, the court within whose jurisdictional area property is situated, the *forum rei sitae*, has jurisdiction to adjudicate claims that will affect rights in such property. Where immovable property is concerned, this court has exclusive jurisdiction to determine its title, claims relating to its transfer, possession or partition, declarations regarding real rights, and declarations that the property is executable. Rescission of contracts for the transfer of immovable property may be heard by the *forum rei sitae* or by a court that has jurisdiction over the defendant,[63] whereas actions concerning immovable property owned by a minor or an incapacitated person may be heard by the *forum domicilii* of that person. The *forum rei sitae* always has jurisdiction in respect of actions relating to the title or delivery of movable property and declarations regarding real rights. It is uncertain whether the *forum domicilii* can also exercise jurisdiction, as was the position in Roman law, and the courts have not yet pronounced on this question. Actions concerning intangible property (e.g., debts, negotiable instruments, shares, and intellectual property) are also heard by the *forum rei sitae*. However, the determination of the situs of such property can be problematic.[64]

88. Interdicts. The legal position regarding interdicts is not clear and, although the rules that follow seem to be generally accepted, it is possible that court decisions may alter them or grant jurisdiction in additional instances. If the respondent is an *incola* of the court, that court will assume jurisdiction to grant both prohibitory and mandatory interdicts, irrespective of where the act is to be performed or restrained.[65] If the respondent is a peregrine, a court will only assume jurisdiction if the requirements for the grant of an interdict are satisfied by facts within the territorial jurisdiction of the High Court.

---

61. *Bid Industrial Holdings (Pty) Ltd v. Strang (Minister of Justice and Constitutional Development, Third Party)* 2008 (3) SA 355 (SCA). This case also confirmed that arrest to found or confirm jurisdiction is unconstitutional.
62. *Veneta Mineraria Spa v. Carolina Collieries (Pty) Ltd* 1987 (4) SA 883 (A).
63. *Hugo v. Wessels* 1987 (3) SA 837 (A).
64. For the various rules that have evolved, *see* C.F. Forsyth, *Private International Law* 219–230 (5th ed., Juta 2012).
65. *Metlika Trading Ltd v. Commissioner South African Revenue Services* 2005 (3) SA 71 (SCA).

89. Actions Affecting Status. Matrimonial Actions. Divorce actions are regulated by statute.[66] A court will have jurisdiction in a divorce action if both parties are, or either of the parties is, domiciled in the area of the court on the date on which action is instituted. A wife is able to obtain a domicile independent of that of her husband. A further ground on which a court may exercise jurisdiction is the ordinary residence within its area on the date of institution of the action[67] by one or both of the parties as well as ordinary residence within the Republic for a period of not less than one year immediately prior to that date. This court will also have jurisdiction in respect of claims in reconvention and counterclaims. A divorce action is defined as including applications *pendente lite* for interdicts, interim orders for maintenance, custody of or access to minor children, and applications for contributions toward costs of the action. The court that has jurisdiction to hear the main action thus automatically has jurisdiction to hear such applications. The Divorce Act also grants this court jurisdiction to make maintenance orders to former spouses and make maintenance, custody, guardianship, and access orders in respect of minor children. Claims for rescission, variation or suspension of custody, guardianship or maintenance orders should, in terms of the common law, also be heard by the court that originally granted the order. However, the Divorce Act provides that a court other than the court that made the original order may alter the order if the parties are, or the applicant is, domiciled in its area.[68] Where the original order was made by a foreign court, the court where the minor is present has jurisdiction. The Act also provides that the court granting a decree of divorce may order a division of assets in accordance with a written agreement between the parties or, in the absence of such an agreement, order that assets belonging to one spouse be transferred to the other. This court may also order forfeiture of the patrimonial benefits of the marriage. If, however, the property includes immovables situated abroad, the court where the property is situated will be viewed as having exclusive jurisdiction. Where claims sounding in money, other than those for maintenance or costs, exist, the court having jurisdiction to hear the divorce action will not, on that ground alone, also be viewed as having jurisdiction to hear the money claim, and the usual principles concerning money claims must be applied.

90. The Divorce Act does not apply to nullity actions, and common law principles must be followed in these instances. A distinction is made between void marriages, where no marriage ever subsisted, and voidable marriages, which are valid until set aside. Marriages are void if the parties are within the prohibited degrees of relationship, if one of the parties is already married, if there was lack of consent by either party or if there was non-compliance with the prescribed formalities. They are voidable where the parent or guardian did not consent to the marriage of a minor, if either spouse is impotent, if the wife was pregnant by another man at the time of marriage or where a party was coerced into the marriage. Although there is no South African case law on the point, it has been suggested that the *lex loci celebrationis* should be used to determine whether a marriage is void, while voidability should be determined by the husband's domiciliary law. A marriage may be declared void by the court in whose area the

66. Section 2(1) Divorce Act 70 of 1979.
67. Section 1(2) of the Divorce Act 70 of 1979 provides that action is deemed instituted on the date on which summons is issued or notice of motion filed.
68. Section 8(2) Divorce Act 70 of 1979.

purported marriage was celebrated or by a court where either the plaintiff or the defendant is domiciled. A marriage may only be declared voidable by the court where either spouse is domiciled.

91. Insolvency. Jurisdiction to order sequestration is regulated by statute.[69] Any High Court has jurisdiction over a debtor and his or her property if the debtor is domiciled or has property situated within the area of the court on the date on which an application for surrender or sequestration is lodged with the registrar, or if the debtor carried on business or resided within the court's area at any time within twelve months immediately preceding the lodging of the application. Foreign sequestration does not automatically bar proceedings in South Africa. Jurisdiction in respect of rehabilitation proceedings is not dealt with by the Act, and the common law rule is that only the court that ordered sequestration is competent to grant a rehabilitation order.

92. The winding-up of companies is also regulated by statute.[70] A court has jurisdiction over a domestic company if either its registered office or main place of business is situated within the area. A court has jurisdiction to order winding-up of a foreign company that does not have the status of an external company if it has a place of business in South Africa.

II. Lower Courts

93. The territorial jurisdiction of lower courts is statutorily regulated, and common law is not taken into account except where the relevant statute is silent or unclear. Each lower court has jurisdiction over a demarcated district and the question of which particular court enjoys territorial jurisdiction is only considered once it has been determined that a lower court can exercise subject matter jurisdiction. No distinction is made between types of claim and, if permitted by the Act, a court will have jurisdiction irrespective of the type of claim. The Magistrates' Courts Act provides that a court will have jurisdiction over the following: a defendant who resides, carries on business or is employed within the district; a defendant partnership that has business premises situated or any member of which resides in the district; any person in respect of proceedings incidental to an action instituted in the court by such person; any person if the cause of action arose wholly within the district (the courts have interpreted this to mean that all the facts in issue must have occurred within the district); any party to interpleader proceedings if the execution creditor and all claimants or a 'third party' reside, carry on business or are employed in the district, if the subject matter of the proceedings has been attached or if the parties consent; any defendant who appears and does not object to the jurisdiction of the court; actions in terms of the Close Corporation Act 69 of 1984; any person who owns immovable property within the district in actions in respect of such property or in respect of mortgage bonds thereon.[71] The Act also authorizes such courts to order attachment of the property of a person who does not reside in South Africa in order to found or confirm jurisdiction. The Act does not detail the various circumstances under which this can occur and High Court

69. Section 149 Insolvency Act 24 of 1936.
70. Section 23 Companies Act 71 of 2008.
71. Section 28(1) Magistrates' Courts Act 32 of 1944.

practice is followed. Similar provisions exist in respect of Small Claims Courts,[72] although these courts are not authorized to found or confirm jurisdiction by attachment.

§3. Resolution of Jurisdiction Conflicts

94. No special court exists to determine jurisdictional conflicts. The Constitution gives the Constitutional Court the power to decide whether something is a constitutional matter. In respect of non-constitutional issues, the court that is approached to hear the matter itself determines whether it is vested with jurisdiction. If a party is aggrieved by this decision, it may appeal to a higher court. An objection to the jurisdiction of a court is raised by a special plea, which is usually decided before the merits of the action are considered. If a court holds that it does not have jurisdiction, the action will be dismissed and must be instituted afresh in a competent court, while, if the plea of jurisdiction is not upheld, the action continues. If more than one court has jurisdiction in respect of a matter, it is the plaintiff's prerogative, as *dominus litis*, to elect the court in which he or she wishes to institute action. However, even if a court has jurisdiction, it may decline to exercise it because it is more convenient for the matter to be heard by another court. The Superior Courts Act provides that, if a matter has been instituted in one court and it appears that the matter may be more conveniently or fittingly heard in another, the first court may, on application by one of the parties and after hearing all the parties concerned, order the matter to be removed to that other court.[73] Similar provisions exist in respect of proceedings in Magistrates' Courts, where the court will consider the expense and inconvenience to the parties. Provisions also exist for the transfer of a matter from a Magistrate's Court to the relevant High Court, at the request of a party.[74]

72. Section 14 Small Claims Courts Act 61 of 1984.
73. Section 27 Superior Courts Act 10 of 2013.
74. Sections 35(1) and 50 Magistrates' Courts Act 32 of 1944.

Chapter 2. International Jurisdiction

§1. Rules Applicable in the Absence of a Treaty

95. South African interpretations of the principles of public international law are conservative, and it is accepted that the State can only enforce its authority within its own territorial area. The only principle of public international law which South African courts recognize for the exercise of civil jurisdiction is that of territoriality, in accordance with which the courts will exercise jurisdiction over persons, property, and causes of action if they have some connection with the territorial area. The courts do not permit the indirect exercise of authority in the territory of another State and will not grant orders that must be enforced or executed outside the country, irrespective of whether the persons who must give effect to such orders are *incolae* of their jurisdictional area.

96. The principle of immunity also affects the exercise of territorial jurisdiction. Foreign States enjoy immunity in respect of acts of State but not in respect of commercial transactions. The position is governed by the Foreign States Immunities Act 87 of 1981, which provides that a foreign State is immune from the civil jurisdiction of South African courts except where:

- It has expressly waived immunity.
- The proceedings relate to a commercial transaction performed by the foreign State or an obligation incurred by it in terms of a contract to be performed within South Africa.
- The proceedings relate to a contract of employment between the foreign State and an individual who was a South African citizen when the contract was concluded or was ordinarily resident in South Africa and not a citizen of the foreign State when action was instituted. The contract must have been entered into or the work must have been performed in South Africa. However, if the proceedings relate to the employment of diplomatic or consular staff, the State enjoys immunity.
- The proceedings relate to the death or injury of a person, or damage or loss of property caused by an act in South Africa.
- The proceedings relate to any interest in, possession or use of, or obligation arising from the foregoing, immovable property in South Africa other than property used as diplomatic mission or consular post. The State also does not enjoy immunity where proceedings relate to an interest arising by way of succession, gift or *bona vacantia* in movable or immovable property.
- The proceedings relate to any patent, trademark, design or plant breeders' right registered or applied for in South Africa belonging to the State, any infringement proceedings in respect thereof or any right to use a trade or business name in South Africa.
- The foreign State is a member of an association or partnership that has members who are not foreign states and that has been established or is controlled in South

Africa, and the proceedings relate to the foreign State's membership of the association.

- The foreign State has agreed in writing to refer a dispute to arbitration and the proceedings relate to the arbitration.
- In the case of admiralty jurisdiction, in an action in rem against a ship belonging to the foreign State, or in an action in personam to enforce a claim in connection with the ship, if the ship was used for commercial purposes.
- The proceedings relate to the foreign State's liability for sales tax, customs or excise duty, or rates in respect of premises used for commercial purposes.

§2. International Treaties

97. No international treaties have been ratified that affect the exercise of international jurisdiction in civil matters in South Africa.

Part III. Actions and Claims

Chapter 1. Actions

§1. Definition

98. Historically, the word 'action' meant the right to enforce a claim in a court of law.[75] However, in modern South African law, this word has a specific legal meaning. In a broad sense, it refers to any form of legal proceeding, while in a narrow sense, it refers to a specific form of proceeding commenced by the issue of summons.[76] The concept discussed here would be referred to in South Africa as a legal right, which has been defined as 'an interest conferred by, and protected by the law, entitling one person to claim that another person or persons either give him or her something, or do an act for him or her, or refrain from doing an act'.[77]

99. Legal subjects (anyone subject to the norms of the law and therefore the bearer of rights and duties) have rights against one another in respect of the objects of their rights (anything to which a right can be had). The following objects of rights are distinguished: things (real rights), performances (personal rights), personality property (right of personality), and industrial property (industrial property rights). However, not every right is legally enforceable, in that it gives rise to a justiciable dispute that a court of law will adjudicate. The fundamental rights contained in Chapter 2 of the Constitution include the right of every person to have any dispute that can be settled by the application of law decided in a fair public hearing before a court or, where appropriate, another independent and impartial forum.[78] In the context of civil procedure, this fundamental right entails access to a court of law, not some other forum.

75. *Actio nihil aliud est, quam ius persequendi iudicio quod sibi debetur* (Inst. 4.6 pr; *cf.* D. 44.7.51) an action is nothing more than the right to enforce a claim in court for what is owing to one: translation by V.G. Hiemstra & H.L. Gonin, *Trilingual Legal Dictionary* 152 (3rd ed., Juta 1992).
76. *Collett v. Priest* 1931 AD 290.
77. D. Hutchison et al., *Wille's Principles of South African Law* 38 (8d ed., Juta).
78. Section 34 Constitution of the Republic of South Africa 1996.

§2. Admissibility

100. Before a court will enforce a right, the claimant must be a legal subject who has the status to litigate. The nature of the right must also render it enforceable.

I. Legal Subjects and Status

101. A legal subject is any entity with the capacity to be the bearer of rights and powers and to be bound by obligations. This concept includes both natural persons and juristic persons. A natural person becomes a legal subject at birth and his or her legal personality terminates at death. A juristic person becomes a legal subject immediately it comes into existence. This is usually effected by legislation, either by separate legislative enactment or in terms of a general enabling enactment. However, the common law also recognizes associations that enjoy juristic personality, provided that they: continue to exist despite any changes in membership; possess or are able to possess property, which belongs to the association and to which the individual members have no right of ownership; are not profit-making associations.

102. A legal subject's status is determined by law, more particularly the law of his or her domicile. His or her status determines the extent to which he or she can participate in legal affairs, that is, his or her legal capacity. Legal capacity in this broad sense includes the capacity to be the bearer of rights and duties (passive legal capacity), the capacity to perform legal acts to which juristic consequences attach (active legal capacity), and the capacity to appear in court as party to an action (capacity to litigate or *locus standi in iudicio*). A legal subject without *locus standi* requires representation or assistance to institute action.

103. Persons with limited or no capacity to litigate:

- *Minors*: a natural person under the age of 18 has no *locus standi* and must be represented or assisted by a legal guardian or, where he or she has no guardian, a curator *ad litem*.
- *Married persons*: the common law marital power of a husband over his wife has been abolished.[79] However, it remains necessary to state a woman's marital status in a High Court summons.[80] Spouses married in community of property must usually obtain the written consent of the other before instituting or defending litigation.
- *Mentally incapacitated persons*: such persons require a curator *ad litem* to litigate on their behalf, as they have no *locus standi*. Prodigals and insolvents have limited legal capacity. Certain categories of person are prohibited from instituting action in any court. Neither a fugitive from justice nor a person who voluntarily resides or carries on business in enemy territory while a war is in progress may institute action in a South African court.

---

79. Section 11 Matrimonial Property Act 88 of 1984.
80. Uniform Rule 17(4).

II. Nature of the Right

104. Where a person acts in a representative capacity, he or she must show that, although not holder of the right, he or she is legally authorized to act on behalf of the holder. This can result from the legal relationship between the parties (e.g., a parent or the trustee of an estate) or from a contractual relationship (e.g., an agent). Where a person holds limited rights, such as a lessee or a recorded user of intellectual property rights, the admissibility of the action is affected.

105. South African common law requires that a party to litigation must have a direct and substantial interest in the right that is the subject matter of the litigation, and in the outcome of the litigation.[81] This interest need not be quantifiable in monetary terms, but it must not be merely abstract or academic. It must also be immediate; a right that might arise at some future stage is not viewed as sufficient interest.[82] A private person cannot make use of the *actio popularis* because the interest is not viewed as sufficiently direct.[83] Class actions are recognized in limited circumstances. The Constitution has altered the common law position when an infringement of or a threat to any fundamental right entrenched in Chapter 2 of the Constitution is alleged. In such instances, any of the following persons are entitled to apply to a competent court for relief: persons acting in their own interest; an association acting in the interest of its members; a person acting on behalf of another person who is not in a position to seek such relief in his or her own name; a person acting as a member of or in the interest of a group or class of persons; a person acting in the public interest. Such a person is known as an amicus curiae and must obtain the consent of other parties before the court to intervene or, failing that, the permission of the Chief Justice. He or she may lodge written argument, which must raise new contentions that may be useful to the court.[84] Where other rights are threatened, the High Court must be approached to certify a class action before it may be instituted. The following seven requirements must be satisfied: a class definition; a cause of action raising a triable issue; common issues of fact or law; the relief sought must be ascertainable and capable of determination; an appropriate procedure for the allocation of damages; a suitable representative; and the class action must be the most appropriate means of determining the claims.[85]

106. In certain circumstances, a person can become a party to litigation without himself or herself exercising that choice. Two such instances exist, known as joinder and third-party procedure. At common law, it was not possible for different plaintiffs with different claims against the same defendant, to institute one action, nor for a plaintiff to sue different defendants, liable for different claims, in one summons. The position has been statutorily amended and joinder is possible in circumstances where the right to relief depends on the determination of substantially the same question of

81. *Jacobs v. Waks* 1992 (1) SA 521 (A).
82. But *see* para. 302 in which declaratory orders are discussed.
83. *Wood v. Ondangwa Tribal Authority* 1975 (2) SA 294 (A).
84. Section 38 Constitution of the Republic of South Africa Act 108 of 1996; Constitutional Court Rule 10.
85. *Children's Resource Centre Trust v. Pioneer Foods (Pty) Ltd* 2013 (2) SA 213 (SCA) paras 26, 28.

law or fact that would arise in each action if separate actions were instituted.[86] When the constitutional validity of a law is challenged, joinder of the national or provincial executive responsible for the administration of that law must also take place. A court may also require joinder of a third person to the proceedings, in terms of the common law, if an order made by the court cannot be carried into effect without prejudicing that person. Third-party procedure may be used when a party claims that he or she is entitled to a contribution or indemnity from a third party in respect of any payment he or she might be ordered to make, or when a matter in dispute is substantially the same as that which will arise between him or her and the third party. In such circumstances, service of a third-party notice has the effect that the third party becomes a party to the action.[87]

107. Finally, in certain instances a person may have a legal right that cannot be enforced against a specific defendant. Heads of foreign states and diplomatic representatives are generally immune from the jurisdiction of the courts.[88] Civil proceedings may not be instituted against a Judge of the High Court without the consent of the head of the court concerned.[89]

108. It is not always statutorily required for a legal representative to hold a written power of attorney before he or she may act on behalf of a litigant. In the Constitutional Court, it is only necessary to file a power of attorney, signed by the party concerned, when the authority of the legal representative is challenged. In High Court proceedings, it is only necessary to file a power of attorney when prosecuting or defending an appeal, but not when instituting or defending an action. However, if the mandate of a legal representative is challenged, proof thereof must be given. The position is similar in Magistrates' Courts.[90]

§3. Vexatious Litigation

109. Even if a person has the capacity to litigate and can show *locus standi*, he or she can be barred from instituting action in certain circumstances in terms of common law or statute. At common law, a court has the inherent power to prevent an abuse of its process and may make an order prohibiting further litigation without its leave where there has been persistent and repeated litigation. However, this power does not extend to preventing a litigant from instituting proceedings in any court against any person. The statutory prohibition is wider in ambit and therefore more frequently used. It provides that a High Court may prohibit a specific person from instituting legal proceedings against any person in both superior and lower courts without the leave of the court concerned. Before it will grant such an order, the court must be satisfied that the person has persistently and without reasonable grounds repeatedly instituted litigation. The order may prohibit the institution of proceedings for an indefinite period, or for such period as the court determines. Subsequent to such an order, a court will

86. Uniform Rule 10, 10A.
87. Uniform Rule 13.
88. Section 4 Diplomatic Immunities and Privileges Act 37 of 2001.
89. Section 47 Superior Courts Act 10 of 2013.
90. Constitutional Court Rule 9; Uniform Rule 7; Magistrates' Courts Rule 52(2).

only grant leave to institute proceedings if satisfied that the intended proceedings are not an abuse of process, and that there are prima facie grounds for the proceedings.[91]

91. Section 2(1) Vexatious Proceedings Act 3 of 1956.

Chapter 2. Claims and Defences

§1. Definition

110. As shown above, the fact that a party has a legal right or right of action does not necessarily entitle him or her to institute legal proceedings, unless he or she also has *locus standi in iudicio* and the court will exercise jurisdiction. Once these two requirements have been met, he or she may, if he or she chooses, claim relief by approaching the appropriate court. However, a party is never compelled to institute legal proceedings even though he or she may have a legal right. Should he or she decide to institute proceedings, this is done by the party, in his or her capacity as plaintiff, issuing summons or, in his or her capacity as applicant, filing a notice of motion. The party against whom proceedings are instituted may then defend the proceedings by, as defendant, noting a plea or, as respondent, filing an answering affidavit.

§2. Distinctions

111. Irrespective of the type of claim, the parties concerned must always be identified and described; their *locus standi* must be apparent and the basis of the court's jurisdiction must be apparent. The object of the claim – that is, the relief sought – must also be set out in full. The nature of the claim determines the form of proceeding that will be used to enforce the claim and the particularity with which the cause of action must be described. Thus, if no dispute of fact exists, application procedure may be used. Here, the parties are identified and the relief set out in the notice of motion, while a full description of the parties and the cause of action is contained in the founding affidavit. If a claim is liquid, provisional sentence procedure may be used, where all the information appears in the summons and the cause of action is stated briefly. If the claim is liquidated, simple summons procedure is used. All information is contained in the summons, in which the cause of action must be set out in concise terms and, if defended, subsequently amplified in the declaration. Unliquidated claims are instituted by combined summons procedure. The summons merely contains the names of the parties, while the particulars of claim annexed to the summons must set out the nature of the claim, a clear and concise statement of the material facts on which the plaintiff relies, the legal conclusions deduced from the material facts and details of the relief claimed. From the above it is clear that it is not the legal basis of the claim, but the nature of the relief claimed and the type of evidence required to prove the claim that determines the choice of procedure.

112. The above distinction relates to procedure in the High Court and in Magistrates' Courts. In Small Claims Courts, only one form of procedure is available, irrespective of the claim.

I. Main Claim

A. *Action Procedure*

113. In all instances, a pleading containing a claim must include a clear and concise statement of the material facts upon which the pleader relies for his or her claim. However, the legal basis of the claim determines the facts that must be averred to support the claim. The rules relating to pleadings set out the following specific instances:[92]

- *Contract*: a party relying on a contract must state whether it is written or oral; when, where and by whom it was concluded; and if written, a true copy of the contract must be annexed to the pleading.
- *Divorce*: where time, date or place or any other person is relevant or involved, details must be given. If division, transfer or forfeiture of assets in respect of a marriage out of community of property is claimed, details must be given of the grounds on which this entitlement is claimed.
- *Damages*: damages must be set out in such a manner that the defendant may reasonably assess the quantum. Where damages for personal injury are claimed, a plaintiff must specify his or her date of birth; the nature and extent of the injuries; and the nature, effects, and duration of the disability alleged to give rise to the damages. He or she must also state separately the amounts claimed for medical costs, pain and suffering, loss of earnings, disability in respect of the enjoyment of the amenities of life, and disfigurement. A claim for damages resulting from the death of another must include the dates of birth of both the deceased and the claimant.

Where a party seeks relief in respect of several distinct claims founded upon separate and distinct facts, such facts and claims must be separately and distinctly stated.[93]

B. *Motion Procedure*

114. The founding affidavit must contain the following information relating to the claim: sufficient details concerning the parties to establish their identities and their *locus standi*; an allegation that the court has jurisdiction; and the grounds on which the applicant relies for the grant of relief. Because an application is decided on the papers and no oral evidence is presented, the founding affidavit must contain not only sufficient facts to disclose a cause of action, but also all the evidence on which the applicant relies.[94]

92. *See* Uniform Rule 18.
93. Uniform Rule 20(3).
94. *See* Uniform Rule 6.

II. Alternative Claims

115. All claims that are contradictory must be pleaded in the alternative, as they will otherwise be excipiable.

III. Counterclaims

116. A defendant may, together with his or her plea, deliver a counterclaim, also known as a claim in reconvention.[95] The material facts must be set out in accordance with the general requirements detailed above in respect of main claims. The counterclaim may be contained in a separate document or in a portion of the document containing the plea. The counterclaim may be conditional on the claim or defence in convention failing. If a defendant alleges that the plaintiff's claim will be extinguished in whole or in part, by the giving of judgment on his or her counterclaim, he or she may in his or her plea refer to the counterclaim and request that judgment on that portion of the plaintiff's claim which would be extinguished by the counterclaim, be postponed until judgment on the counterclaim is given. A counterclaim is a convenient alternative to the institution of a separate action by the defendant against the plaintiff. It has the advantage that the plaintiff cannot object to the jurisdiction of the court and that the two claims are determined simultaneously, and judgment entered for the balance. The relief claimed in the counterclaim need not be related to the relief claimed in the main claim.

IV. Defence

A. Action Procedure

117. Two types of defence may be raised, a plea on the merits that deals with the merits of the plaintiff's claim and a special plea that raises a defence on the basis of facts that do not appear in the plaintiff's pleading.

118. Plea on the merits: in this plea, the defendant must admit, deny, place in issue, or confess and avoid all the material facts alleged by the plaintiff. The defendant must also clearly and concisely state all the material facts on which he or she relies. Every factual allegation by the plaintiff that is not denied or placed in issue is deemed to be admitted. If an explanation or qualification of a denial is necessary, this must also be stated in the plea.[96]

119. Special plea: this does not deal with the merits of the action but alleges special facts unconnected with the merits as a result of which the action is destroyed or postponed. Examples of dilatory pleas that will postpone the action are pleas of *lis alibi pendens*, the questioning of the plaintiff's authority to sue and pleas relying on an arbitration agreement. Examples of pleas in abatement, which destroy the action,

95. Uniform Rules 22(4) and 24.
96. Uniform Rule 22.

are pleas of prescription, non-joinder, res iudicata, and pleas to the jurisdiction of the court.

B. Motion Procedure

120. In an answering affidavit, the respondent must state which of the applicant's allegations he or she admits and which he or she denies. The respondent must also set out his or her version of the relevant facts. Due to the nature of these proceedings, a bare denial is insufficient, and the respondent must deal more fully with allegations made by the applicant than is the equivalent position in action procedure.

Chapter 3. Sanctions on Procedural Irregularities

§1. Formal Requirements

121. The primary mechanism in the High Court used to object to a procedural irregularity is contained in Uniform Rule 30, which provides that a party to a cause in which an irregular step has been taken, may apply to court to have it set aside. The term 'irregular' is not defined in the rules but is viewed as applying only to irregularities of form and not to matters of substance.[97] It can include failure to sign a pleading, use of the incorrect form of summons, premature set down for trial and non-compliance with the rules governing the various pleadings. A party objecting to an irregular step must give written notice to his or her opponent to remove the cause of complaint within ten days of becoming aware of the irregularity. If the irregularity is not corrected within ten days, the objector may apply to court to have the irregular step set aside within the next fifteen days. Such an application may only be brought if the objector has not himself or herself taken some further step in the litigation after becoming aware of the irregularity. A 'further step' has been defined as some act which advances the proceedings one step closer to completion'.[98] The court hearing such an application has the power to set aside, in whole or in part, the irregular step, or to grant leave to amend the pleading to remove the irregularity, or to make any other order it considers fitting. Until the party against whom the order was made has complied with it, he or she may take no further step in the main action.

122. Two further procedures are used to object to the contents of documents or pleadings exchanged between parties. An exception is a legal objection that may be raised to a pleading on the grounds that it is vague and embarrassing, or that it discloses no cause of action or defence.[99] An exception must appear *ex facie* the pleading concerned and no fresh facts may be alleged; the facts contained in the pleading under attack must be accepted as true. Before an exception can be taken to a pleading on the ground that it lacks detail, notice must be given to the other party to remove the cause of complaint. A notice of exception must be delivered within the period allowed for the filing of any subsequent pleading and the grounds on which the exception is founded must be clearly stated in the notice. When the court upholds an exception, only the pleading excepted to is destroyed, not the whole claim or defence. It is therefore a practice to grant the party whose pleading was held excipiable leave to file an amended pleading.

Where a pleading or affidavit contains averments that are scandalous, vexatious or irrelevant, the opposing party may apply to have this matter struck out. Application must be made within the period allowed for filing any subsequent pleading, and the

97. Erasmus *Superior Court Practice* B1-191.
98. *Pettersen v. Burnside* 1940 NPD 403 at 406.
99. Uniform Rule 23(1).

application will only be granted if the court is satisfied that the applicant will otherwise be prejudiced in the conduct of his or her claim or defence.[100]

123. The distinction between these two procedures has been described as follows:

> An exception goes to the root of the entire claim or defence as the case may be. The excipient alleges that the pleading objected to, taken as it stands, is legally invalid for its purpose. Whereas individual sections, which do not comprise the entire claim or defence, but are only portion of one, must if objected to, be attacked by a motion to expunge.[101]

124. The Uniform Rules also provide that the court may, on good cause shown, condone any non-compliance with the rules.[102] This provision gives the courts a wide discretion which they have protected by refraining from defining 'good cause'. However, the applicant for condonation is always required to file an affidavit explaining the reasons for his or her non-compliance. Any non-compliance may be condoned in appropriate circumstances, irrespective of whether the rule concerned is directory or mandatory.

125. The procedure to have an irregular step set aside, to note an exception and to apply for striking out is also available in Magistrates' Courts.[103] In addition, a request for further particulars for purposes of trial is available in Magistrates' Courts.[104] Non-compliance with the rules is not a ground for giving judgment against a party who is in default or has committed a procedural error, unless a specific rule provides otherwise.[105]

126. The Constitutional Court may excuse the parties from compliance with any of its rules, on sufficient cause shown.[106] This court also has a greater leeway in prescribing procedure than other courts and may give directions in matters of practice and procedure as it considers just and expedient. Due to the less formal nature of proceedings in Small Claims Courts, none of the above procedures is available in these courts.

§2. Time Limits

127. Time limits may be specified by legislation or imposed by a court order. If no limit is specified, the act must be performed within a reasonable time. When time limits fixed by legislation or court order are calculated, only court days (i.e., not Saturdays, Sundays or public holidays) are included. When a certain number of days is prescribed for doing an act, it must be calculated exclusive of the first day and

100. Uniform Rule 23(2).
101. *Salzman v. Holmes* 1914 AD 152 at 156.
102. Uniform Rule 27(3).
103. Magistrates' Courts Rules 19(1)–(4), 60(A).
104. Magistrates' Courts Rule 16(2)(a). Both a request for further particulars for purposes of pleading and a request for copies of documents or accounts no longer apply.
105. Magistrates' Courts Rule 60(1)–(4).
106. Constitutional Court Rule 32.

inclusive of the last day.[107] Time limits in the High Court may usually be altered by agreement between the parties. The court may, in the absence of agreement, extend or abridge any time prescribed in either the Uniform Rules or a court order. An application for such an extension may be ordered although the relevant time limit has already expired. The application must be made on notice, and good cause must be shown.[108] The Chief Justice of the Constitutional Court may condone non-compliance with or extend any time limit prescribed in the rules of this court.[109]

128. When a party fails to deliver a pleading within the time laid down in the Uniform Rules, he or she may be barred from doing so.[110] The party will be *ipso facto* barred if he or she fails to deliver a replication or subsequent pleading within the specified time, and the pleadings are then deemed closed. If a party is in default with a prior pleading (i.e., a declaration, plea or exception), a notice of bar must first be served on the defaulting party requiring him or her to deliver the pleading within a specified period. The party is only barred if he or she fails to deliver the pleading within this further period. The days between 16 December and 15 January inclusive are not counted in the time allowed for the delivery of pleadings for purposes of bar. A party may apply to court for removal of the bar.

129. In Magistrates' Courts, periods of time contained in the Act are court days,[111] which is in line with periods of time contained in the rules which are also court days (i.e., Saturdays, Sundays, and public holidays are excluded). The time limits prescribed by the rules, other than those relating to the noting of appeal, may be extended by the written consent of the opposing party or, if consent is refused, by application to the court. The procedure of bar is now available in Magistrates' Courts and if a party does not comply with time limits, an application to court for compliance to be ordered must be made.[112] Provision is now made for automatic bar in Magistrates' Courts.[113] The bar procedure followed is the same as in the High Court. Automatic bar applies in respect of replication and subsequent pleadings. It is triggered in respect of all other pleadings upon a failure to comply.[114]

---

107. Section 4 Interpretation Act 33 of 1957.
108. Uniform Rule 27. Supreme Court of Appeal Rule 11(1)(a) also allows the court to do so *mero motu*.
109. Constitutional Court Rule 1(5).
110. Uniform Rules 26, 27(1).
111. Section 1 of Courts of Law Amendment Act 7 of 2017.
112. Magistrates' Courts Rule 60.
113. Magistrates' Courts Rule 21B. This rule is similar to Uniform Rule 26 in the High Courts.
114. Magistrates' Courts Rules 12(1)(b) and 15(5). *See* Government Gazette 39715 of 19 Feb. 2016 and Government Gazette 40045 of 3 Jun. 2016.

Part IV. Proceedings

Chapter 1. Pretrial Proceedings

130. Before litigation is commenced, it is usual to demand the relief required from the opposing party or give him or her notice of the intention to commence proceedings. Failure to do so can often result in increased costs that cannot be recovered from the other party. However, only in certain circumstances is it essential to give notice. The first instance is where a demand is essential to complete the cause of action, as without a demand, the liability is not complete. Instances where a demand is an essential element of the cause of action are determined by the rules of substantive law and will not be detailed here. Second, it is also necessary to give notice of proceedings when failure to do so would void the proceedings. Such circumstances deal with litigation against State and parastate organs. These provisions make prior notice a requirement and stipulate a period of time within which proceedings must be commenced and which must elapse between receipt of notice and the commencement of proceedings. Such provisions are peremptory and strict compliance is essential. Previously, the courts could not condone non-compliance unless authorized to do so by statute. The constitutionality of such statutory notice requirements and expiry periods was challenged, and the court held that what counted was the sufficiency and adequacy of the notice periods. The Institution of Legal Proceedings against Certain Organs of State Act 40 of 2002 was then introduced to regulate prescription and to harmonize the periods of prescription of claims against statutory organs. Prior to the issue of summons in terms of the Road Accident Fund Act 56 of 1996, a claim must be filed with the fund or an appointed agent. Finally, section 29 of the Small Claims Courts Act 61 of 1984 makes it essential to deliver a written demand to the defendant allowing him or her at least fourteen days to satisfy the claim, prior to the issue of summons in such courts.

131. In two instances, a preliminary application is required before the launch of proceedings. First, when jurisdiction is sought over a peregrine defendant, attachment of his or her property is usually necessary. Prior to the institution of proceedings, an application must be made to the court that will hear the proceedings for an order permitting attachment. Second, when substituted service or edictal citation will be the method used to give the defendant notice of the proceedings, a preliminary application for permission to do so is also necessary.[115]

115. *See* in this regard para. 134.

Chapter 2. Proceedings in First Instance

§1. Adversary Proceedings

I. Ordinary Proceedings

A. Introduction of the Claim

1. Notice

132. It is a fundamental principle of our legal system that a person is entitled to notice of any proceedings instituted against him or her.[116] The Constitutional Court rules allow notice to be given by registered post, facsimile or electronic copy. In High Court proceedings, notice is ensured by having the sheriff serve the document initiating proceedings on the defendant and requiring the sheriff to furnish a return of service containing details of how service was effected. All High Court process directed to the sheriff (i.e., all summonses, writs, subpoenas, and notices of motion which commence application proceedings, other than those commencing interlocutory applications where the party is represented by an attorney of record) require service by the sheriff. All other processes can be delivered to a party at his or her address for service. The electronic era has impacted on service of documents through the electronic medium. It should be noted that summonses, writs and other processes may now be transmitted by fax or any other electronic medium in civil proceedings before a Superior Court.[117] The document received or printed will have the same force as the original.

133. Where the party is within South Africa and his or her whereabouts are known, the sheriff should if possible serve process on the party personally; where this is not possible, process may be served at his or her place of employment, residence or *domicilium citandi*. The party's authorized agent may also accept service on his or her behalf. The sheriff must explain the nature and contents of the document to the party on whom service is effected and must state that this has been done in his or her return. The return of service is prima facie proof of what is stated therein. Service may take place anywhere within South Africa, and no additional formalities are necessary if service takes place outside the jurisdiction of the court but within the country.

134. If a party is within South Africa but his or her whereabouts are unknown, the court must be approached to give directions on how substituted service must take place. If a party is outside South Africa, he or she must be sued by edictal citation irrespective of whether his or her whereabouts are known or not. Once again, the leave

116. Constitutional Court Rules 1(4), Uniform Rule 4 and Magistrates' Courts Rule 9 contain full details on how service must be effected.

117. Section 44 of Superior Courts Act 10 of 2013. Also *see* s. 40 of the Judicial Matters Amendment Act 8 of 2017. Uniform Rule 4A also provides for service of documents through the electronic medium.

of the court must be obtained. In both instances, an application is brought prior to the main action by the person wishing to cause service to be effected. The application must set out the nature and extent of the claim, the grounds upon which it is based and upon which the court has jurisdiction to hear the matter, and the manner of service that the court is asked to authorize. If the whereabouts of the person are unknown, his or her last known whereabouts and the efforts made to trace him or her must also be detailed. The court will then make an order on the manner in which service must be effected and the time within which notice of intention to defend must be given. When service must be effected outside South Africa, this procedure need only be followed for process that institutes proceedings. Service of other process outside South Africa may be authorized more informally by requesting leave from the court during the hearing of the matter.[118]

135. The procedure for service of process in the Magistrates' Courts is substantially similar to that in Superior Courts. Provision is made for two further methods of service of Magistrates' Courts process that are not available in the High Court. The plaintiff may give the sheriff written instructions to serve process by registered post, in which case the process is posted by prepaid registered post to the defendant's address. An acknowledgement of receipt is included. The other method that may be used if service cannot otherwise be effected is the affixing of the process to the door of the defendant's residence or place of business. A Magistrate's Court may also authorize substituted service and edictal citation. The electronic era has also impacted on service of documents in Magistrates' Courts. Service of a notice, request, statement or any other document that is not a process, may be effected by hand or by registered post, or may be sent by fax or electronic mail.[119]

136. In Small Claims Courts, the procedure is much simpler. The plaintiff may deliver the summons to the defendant or request the sheriff to do so.

2. Registration by the Court

137. The registrar of the Constitutional Court must number and file all process lodged at his or her office.[120] Prior to the service of a High Court summons, it must be signed and issued by the registrar of the relevant division and made returnable to the court through him or her. A different procedure is followed in respect of application proceedings, where service is first effected and the notice of motion thereafter filed with the registrar. A substantially similar procedure is followed in Magistrates' Courts, where the clerk of the court is the official who controls the issue of process. In Small Claims Courts, the clerk of the court must be satisfied that prior written demand has been given before he or she will issue a summons.

118. Full details of the manner in which proof of service outside South Africa must be furnished and authenticated are contained in Uniform Rules 4(7) and 63, and Magistrates' Courts Rule 10.

119. Magistrates' Courts Rule 9(9)(a).

120. Constitutional Court Rule 4; Uniform Rules 6(4)(a), 17(3); Magistrates' Courts Rule 3; s. 29 Small Claims Courts Act 61 of 1984.

3. Summary Judgment

138. Summary judgment is available in both the High Court and Magistrates' Courts in certain instances where an abuse of the process of court might otherwise occur.[121] This procedure grants a final judgment without a trial in instances where a defence has allegedly been raised merely to delay the recovery by the plaintiff of the relief he or she seeks. The procedure impinges on the defendant's right to have his or her case heard and even if the plaintiff is able to show that he or she has an indefensible case, the court retains discretion to grant or refuse summary judgment.

139. In both courts, summary judgment may only be sought in respect of the following claims: on a liquid document (i.e., a document where the indebtedness is acknowledged in a fixed and definite sum);[122] for a liquidated sum of money (i.e., an amount capable of prompt and speedy ascertainment); for delivery of specified movable property and for ejectment. Any claim for interest or costs arising from the claim may also be granted.

140. Summary judgment may only be requested by the plaintiff after the defendant has filed a notice of intention to defend on receipt of a summons containing a claim of the nature set out above. The plaintiff must use the application procedure and serve the application on the defendant within fifteen days after receipt of the notice of intention to defend. A plaintiff may waive his or her right to apply for summary judgment if he or she takes a further procedural step before applying for summary judgment. The notice of motion must be accompanied by an affidavit in which the plaintiff, or anyone else who can swear positively to the facts, verifies the cause of action and the amount claimed and states that in his or her opinion the defendant has no bona fide defence, and that the notice of intention to defend has been filed merely for the purpose of delay. The affidavit must not contain evidence of the facts supporting the plaintiff's case. If the claim is based on a liquid document, a copy must be annexed to the affidavit. The notice must state that the application will be set down for hearing on a stated day not less than ten days from delivery of the notice. The procedure to be followed by the plaintiff if such an application is launched in a Magistrate's Court is identical, except that the time within which the application must be launched is fifteen days, and no affidavit need be filed if the claim is based on a liquid document, a copy of the document being sufficient.

141. On receipt of the application, the defendant may give security to satisfy the judgment, including costs. The court will then grant leave to defend the main action, which proceeds as if no application for summary judgment had been launched. Alternately, the defendant may satisfy the court that he or she does have a bona fide defence. This may be done by filing an affidavit before the date of hearing or, with the leave of the court, giving oral evidence to this effect. Neither party may cross-examine a person who gives oral or affidavit evidence, although the court may question a person giving oral evidence. The affidavit or oral evidence must disclose fully the nature and grounds of the defence and the material facts relied on therefor. Although the defence need not be set out with the precision necessary in a subsequent plea, it must be formulated clearly enough to enable the court to determine whether it constitutes a

121. *See* Uniform Rule 32 and Magistrates' Courts Rule 14.
122. *See* para. 217 for a fuller discussion of this term.

real defence. If the defendant satisfies the court that he or she has a bona fide defence, the court grants him or her leave to defend the action. If he or she cannot convince the court that he or she has a bona fide defence, the court may in its discretion grant summary judgment. An order for costs may be used to penalize a party whose application was unfounded or whose defence appears during the main action to have been unreasonable.

142. Summary judgment is not available in Small Claims Courts.

B. Progress of Proceedings

143. In the Constitutional Court, all litigation is in the form of application proceedings, either ex parte or on notice.

144. Three forms of proceeding exist in the High Court and Magistrates' Courts. Action (illiquid summons) procedure is used when a material dispute of fact exists, and the claim is either liquidated or unliquidated. Liquid (provisional sentence) procedure is used when provisional sentence is sought, and the claim is based on a liquid document. Application (motion) procedure, either on notice or ex parte, is used when no material dispute of fact exists. Provisional sentence procedure is discussed in paragraphs 215–221 only the illiquid summons and motion procedures will be dealt with here.

1. Exchange of Pleadings: Illiquid Summons Procedure

145. The action or illiquid summons procedure is characterized by a marked difference between the pleading and trial stages.[123] A specified number of written pleadings, intended to formulate and define the issues the court must consider, are exchanged between the parties to the action. After pleadings have closed, the trial commences with the presentation of oral evidence to support the parties' allegations.

146. Various general rules apply to all pleadings. Pleadings must state facts and not law. Evidence may not be included in a pleading. Only material, admissible facts may be pleaded. These facts must be alleged clearly and concisely and must be stated in summary form. However, the pleading must have sufficient particularity not to be vague and embarrassing. Material facts which appear in another party's pleading must be dealt with. Inconsistent allegations may only appear in the alternative. Certain formal requirements also exist. All pleadings must be signed by the party concerned, if acting for himself or herself, otherwise by an advocate or a duly admitted attorney in the High Court and by an attorney in Magistrates' Court proceedings. Pleadings must be divided into consecutively numbered paragraphs. All pleadings and documents must be clearly printed or type-written on one side only of A4 size paper.

147. In the High Court, two types of summons may be used to commence illiquid summons proceedings. Combined summons are used for unliquidated claims, whereas simple summons are used when the claim is based on a debt or liquidated demand. A debt or liquidated demand is interpreted as a monetary claim capable of speedy ascertainment, while an unliquidated claim is any other type of monetary claim where the court must determine quantum and claims affecting status. Both types of summons

123. *See* Uniform Rules 17–20, 22, 24–25 and 29.

must be in accordance with prescribed forms.[124] The simple summons sets out the cause of action briefly in the body of the summons, while the combined summons contains a separate statement of the material facts known as the particulars of claim. Both summonses must contain the following: a description of the parties, an address for service and the time within which appearance to defend must be entered. The simple summons is supplemented, after entry of appearance, by a pleading known as the declaration, which in content corresponds to the particulars of claim annexed to the combined summons. Both these pleadings must set out the nature of the plaintiff's claim, a statement of the material facts on which he or she relies in support of the claim, the conclusions of law which he or she is entitled to deduce from these facts, and a prayer for the relief claimed. Specific information that must be included in these pleadings in respect of divorce actions, claims based on contract and claims for damages are detailed in the Uniform Rules.

148. If the defendant wishes to oppose the action, a notice of intention to defend must be delivered to the registrar and the plaintiff or his or her attorney. This must be done within the period set out in the summons. The notice must contain the defendant's full residential address and his or her address for service. If action is commenced by simple summons, the plaintiff must then file a declaration. Hereafter, the sequence of events is the same irrespective of the type of summons used.

149. The defendant must deliver a plea within a specified period. In his or her plea, the defendant must admit or deny or confess and avoid all the material facts alleged in the particulars of claim or declaration, or he or she must state which of the facts are not admitted and to what extent. The defendant must also clearly and concisely state all material facts upon which he or she relies. Every allegation of fact in the particulars of claim or declaration that is not expressly denied or not admitted is deemed to be admitted. The defendant may deliver a claim in reconvention setting out the material facts supporting his or her counterclaim together with a plea. The defendant may also, rather than delivering a plea on the merits, deliver a special plea. This plea does not raise a defence on the merits of the plaintiff's claim as set out in the declaration or particulars of claim, but on the basis of facts that do not appear in these pleadings; it has the effect of destroying or postponing the plaintiff's action.

150. The plaintiff may reply to the defendant's plea by delivering a replication. This is not an essential pleading and is not necessary where it would merely serve to join issue or deny allegations in the plea. However, it should be delivered where the plea requires new allegations. If a counterclaim has been instituted, the plaintiff must at this stage also deliver a plea in reconvention, which must comply with the rules governing the plea. Further pleadings, both in convention and reconvention, may be delivered if necessary.

151. Pleadings are considered closed if either party has joined issue without alleging new matter and without adding any further pleading or if the last day for filing a replication or subsequent pleading has elapsed without it being filed. The parties can also agree that pleadings are considered closed or apply to court to declare them closed if agreement cannot be reached.

152. The sequence of pleadings in the Magistrates' Courts is almost identical.[125]

124. Form 9 (simple summons), form 10 (combined summons) Sch. 1 Uniform Rules.
125. *See* Magistrates' Courts Rules 5, 15–16, 17, 20–21.

153. In Small Claims Courts, the only necessary pleading is the summons, which must be preceded by a letter of demand. The defendant may, however, provide a written statement setting out his or her defence to the court and the plaintiff at any time before the hearing of the case.[126]

2. Other Preparatory Measures

154. During the course of litigation, certain steps that might be necessary to prepare for the trial may be taken either before or after the close of pleadings, while other preparatory measures may only be taken after pleadings have been closed. This distinction is important as a step taken before it is procedurally due will be of no effect.

3. Further Particulars

155. In the High Court, further particulars may only be requested after the close of pleadings but not less than twenty days before the trial date. Either party may make such a request.[127] A notice is served on the opposing party in which only further particulars strictly necessary to enable the party making the request to prepare for trial may be sought. The purpose of further particulars is to enable a party to avoid being taken by surprise at the trial and to inform him or her of the allegations he or she will have to counter. However, neither party is entitled to know what evidence the other party will lead. The request must be complied with within ten days. Both the request and the reply must be signed by the party's legal representative. If a reply is not delivered on time or contains insufficient information, the requesting party may apply to court for the delivery of a reply or an amplified reply or for the dismissal of the action or striking out of the defence. The court has a wide discretion as to the order it should make. If further particulars are requested too late (i.e., within twenty days of the trial date), an order compelling delivery thereof cannot be sought.

156. The position is similar in Magistrates' Courts.

157. Further particulars are not available in the Constitutional Court or in Small Claims Courts.

4. Discovery

158. Discovery is the procedure that enables the parties to ascertain what documents and recordings exist that might be relevant to the action.[128,129] This enables a party to prepare fully for trial and avoid being taken by surprise. The existence of documents relating to any issue in question in the action that may advance or disprove either party's case at issue. Our courts have held that documents that tend only to

126. *See* s. 29 Small Claims Courts Act 61 of 1984.

127. *See* Uniform Rule 21 and Magistrates' Courts Rule 16.

128. *See* Uniform Rule 35, Constitutional Court Rule 29 and Magistrates' Courts Rule 23.

129. Tape recordings are referred to in Uniform Rule 35 while Magistrates' Courts Rule 23 refers to tape, electronic, digital or other forms of recording. In the discussion that follows, a reference to a document includes reference to a recording when appropriate.

advance the case of the party making discovery need not be disclosed if they will not be used at the trial.

159. With one exception, discovery can only be requested after close of pleadings. This exception allows a party to request inspection of clearly specified documents for purposes of pleading. It must be shown that the document is relevant to a reasonably anticipated issue in the action. The document must be made available for inspection and copying within five days.

160. In the High Court, after pleadings have closed, any party can serve a notice on another party to the action requiring him or her to make discovery on oath within twenty days of all documents that are or have been in his or her possession or control. An affidavit must be prepared and attested by the party receiving the notice in which the following documents are separately specified: documents in his or her possession or that of his or her agent (this includes his or her attorney) and not specified under the next category; documents in his or her possession that he or she has a valid objection to produce (i.e., privileged documents); and documents that he or she had in the past but that are no longer in his or her possession. A document is considered to be sufficiently specified if described as one of a bundle of documents of a specified nature that have been initialled and consecutively numbered. The following are viewed as privileged and need not be included: witness statements taken for the purpose of the proceedings; communications between attorney-and-client and/or advocate; and pleadings, affidavits, and notices in the action. This list is not exhaustive and any other document considered privileged need not be discovered, although the reason for objecting to its production must be set out. If a document is not disclosed, it may not be used at the trial by the party who was responsible for its non-disclosure, although other parties to the action may use it. If the party who requested discovery believes that certain documents have not been disclosed, he or she may require the party who made discovery to make them available for inspection or to state on oath that they are not in his or her possession, in which case he or she must state their whereabouts if known.

161. After a discovery affidavit has been received, the recipient may request inspection of those documents that are not privileged. The party who made discovery must then file a notice stating a time, within five days, when the documents may be inspected and copied over a period of five days. If a party fails to make discovery or allow inspection, the court can be approached to order compliance; if compliance is not forthcoming, the court may dismiss the claim or strike out the defence.

162. Two further forms of discovery that may be requested after close of pleadings are available. While a discovery notice only relates to documents that have been in a party's possession or control, provision is made first for documents in the control of third parties. In this instance, a party gives notice to any other party to the action to specify particulars of dates and parties of or to any document that is intended to be used at the trial on behalf of such party. The recipient of the notice must, not less than fifteen days before the trial, specify the dates of and parties to, and the general nature of any such documents in his or her possession. He or she must also furnish particulars to identify any such documents not in his or her possession and the name and address of the person in whose possession the documents are. Similar provisions apply in respect of documents referred to in pleadings or affidavits, where the party giving notice must be allowed to inspect and copy such documents. Notice may also be given to a party who has made discovery of a document to produce the original at the hearing. The party who requested production may then hand the document in at the hearing without having to call a witness to identify it.

163. Provision is also made for a party who proposes to prove a document at the trial to avoid the costs attendant on proving it by serving a notice on another party requiring him or her to admit that the document was properly executed and is what it purports to be. If the recipient of the notice refuses to admit the document, it must be proved in the usual way, but he or she may then be ordered to pay the costs of its proof. The court may also order any party under oath to produce a document that is relevant to the action and is in his or her possession.

164. The Constitutional Court rules provide that the Uniform Rule relating to discovery in application proceedings applies *mutatis mutandis*.

165. The position in Magistrates' Courts is similar to that in the High Court. Discovery procedures are not available to litigants in Small Claims Courts.

5. Medical Examinations

166. A party to proceedings in which damages or compensation are claimed in respect of alleged bodily injury has the right to require the party making the claim to submit to medical examination if his or her state of health is relevant to determine the damages or compensation.[130] A similar right also exists where a person claims damages resulting from the death of another person, and it is alleged that his or her own state of health is relevant in determining damages. The examination may be required at any stage of proceedings; it is not necessary to wait for close of pleadings. The notice requiring the person to submit to an examination must specify the nature of the examination, the persons who will conduct it, and the place, date, and time thereof. The notice must also state that the person's own medical adviser may be present at the examination. Although no provision is made for the person's legal adviser to be present, our courts have held that this is permissible. A remittance for the reasonable expenses incurred in attending the examination, calculated on the same scale as for witnesses in civil trials, must accompany the notice.

167. Within five days, the recipient must give written notification of the nature and grounds of any objections he or she has to the nature of the examination, the persons conducting it, the place, date or time of the examination, or the amount of remuneration. If his or her objection is to the place, date or time, the party must suggest an alternative, while if the remuneration is unacceptable, particulars of the amount required must be provided. If no objection is delivered within the five-day period, the recipient is deemed to have agreed to the examination on the terms set out in the notice.

168. If it appears from the medical examination that a further examination is necessary, this may be required in the same manner. The party who requested the examination must obtain a written report from the examiner that sets out fully the results of his or her examination and the opinions he or she formed on any relevant matter. If requested, other parties must be furnished with a complete copy of the report. The party who requested the examination must bear the expense, although this expense

130. *See* Uniform Rule 36(1)–36(5A), 36(8) and Magistrates' Courts Rule 24(1)–24(5A), 24(8).

forms part of his or her costs and may therefore be recovered if a costs order is made in his or her favour after trial.

169. Medical reports, hospital records, X-ray photographs, and other documents of a similar nature may also be requested by notice if they are relevant to assess damages claims in respect of bodily injuries. They must be furnished within ten days.

170. The procedure in the High Court and in Magistrates' Courts is identical. No provision is made for such examinations in respect of proceedings in the Constitutional Court or in Small Claims Courts.

6. Examination of Objects

171. If the state or condition of something may be relevant to the decision of a matter at issue in an action, a party may at any stage of proceedings require the party relying on the existence of such state or having the property in his or her possession or under his or her control, to make it available for inspection or examination.[131] The notice requires the property or a fair sample thereof to remain available for inspection for a period of not more than ten days from receipt thereof. The recipient of the notice may require the nature of the examination to be specified and is not bound to submit the property for examination if this will materially prejudice him or her by reason of the effect thereof on the property. In the event of a dispute over the submission of property for examination, a judge may by notice be requested to determine the dispute. The party causing the examination to be made must obtain a full written report, which must be furnished to other parties on request and must bear the expense of the examination, which forms part of his or her costs.

172. No plan, diagram, model or photograph may be tendered in evidence unless the party intending to do so has given notice not less than fifteen days before the hearing, offering it for inspection, and requiring the party receiving the notice to admit the plan, diagram, model or photograph within ten days. If it is not admitted, it must be proved in the usual manner, but the party refusing admission may be ordered to pay the costs of proof.

173. Identical provisions govern such examinations in both the High Court and in Magistrates' Courts. The procedure is not available in proceedings in Small Claims Courts.

174. The Constitutional Court rules make provision for a more simple procedure.[132] Models, diagrams, and exhibits that form part of the evidence in a case must be brought to the court for inspection and placed in the custody of the registrar at least ten days before the case is heard or submitted. Notification need not be given to other parties.

7. Expert Witnesses

175. Any party who wishes to call an expert witness in a matter where such evidence may be received must deliver notice of his or her intention to do so not less than fifteen days before the trial.[133] A summary of the expert's opinions and his or her

131. *See* Uniform Rule 36(6)–36(8), 36(10) and Magistrates' Courts Rule 24(6)–24(8), 24(10).
132. Constitutional Court Rule 26.
133. *See* Uniform Rule 36(9) and Magistrates' Courts Rule 24(9).

reasons therefore must be delivered not less than ten days before the trial. If this is not done, an expert may only be called with the leave of the court or the consent of all the parties to the action. This provision prevents a party from being taken by surprise and enables each party to prepare before trial to be in a position to answer the other party's expert evidence. It also enables the experts to exchange views and thereby limit the duration of the trial. The provisions in the High Court and in Magistrates' Courts are identical.

8. Pretrial Conference

176. After the close of pleadings in High Court proceedings, the plaintiff's attorney must request the attorneys acting for other parties to the action to attend a conference at a mutually convenient time with the object of reaching agreement as to possible ways of curtailing the duration of the trial.[134] The conference must be held at least six weeks prior to the trial.

177. A list of matters that must be considered is prescribed, including the admissions required, the enquiries that will be made, and other issues regarding preparation for trial. The parties must also discuss the possibility of reaching a settlement of the case. This list of matters is not exhaustive, and parties may discuss and agree on any other relevant matters.

178. The attorneys must draw up and sign a minute of the specified matter that required consideration at the conclusion of the conference and give this to the registrar at least five weeks before the trial. Provision is also made that, before the trial proceeds, a judge may call the parties into his or her chambers with a view to obtaining directions on any matters likely to curtail the duration of the trial. A special costs order may be made against a party for failure to attend the conference or to promote the effective disposal of the litigation. Although it is not compulsory, the advocates for the respective parties are usually also present at the pretrial conference.

179. Provision is also made in the Magistrates' Courts for a conference to curtail trial proceedings. The major distinction between the procedures in the two courts is that in the lower courts the conference is held in the presence of a Magistrate and may take place at any stage of the proceedings. The court may of its own accord or at the written request of one of the parties direct the parties or their representatives to appear before it in chambers to consider: the simplification of the issues; the necessity or desirability of amending the pleadings; the possibility of obtaining admissions of fact or of documents; the limitation of the number of expert witnesses; and any other matters that could dispose of the matter expeditiously and inexpensively. If one of the parties wishes to convene such a conference, he or she must file a notice with the clerk of the court in which a general indication of the matters he or she wishes to have considered is given. The clerk submits this request to a Magistrate who decides whether a conference should be held and, if so, directs the clerk to issue the necessary process. This is effected by sending a letter, signed by the clerk and accompanied by a copy of the notice, to all the parties at least ten days before the conference date. If a party refuses to attend the conference, a costs order may be made against him or her. At the conclusion of

134. *See* Uniform Rule 37, s. 54 of the Magistrates' Courts Act 32 of 1944 and Magistrates' Courts Rule 25.

the conference, the Magistrate makes an order that sets out the action taken at the conference, the amendments allowed to the pleadings and any agreements reached by the parties. The order also limits the issues for trial to those not disposed of by admissions or agreements of the parties. The order is binding on the parties unless altered at the trial to prevent manifestation of injustice.

9. Purely Written Procedure

180. No distinction exists between the pleading and evidence stages in application proceedings. The documents exchanged between the parties formulate the issues of fact and contain the evidence adduced in proof of the factual averments. When the matter is heard in the High Court or in a Magistrate's Court, the hearing consists solely of legal argument by the parties or their legal representatives, and no oral evidence is presented by the parties, except in exceptional circumstances. In the Constitutional Court, the Chief Justice may give directions as to how the application should be dealt with and whether it should be set down for hearing or dealt with on the basis of written argument or summarily on the basis of information contained in the affidavits.[135] Application proceedings can be on notice to other parties, or ex parte, when no notification of the proceedings need be given. Only proceedings on notice will be discussed here, as ex parte proceedings are dealt with in paragraphs 228–230.

181. In the High Court, application proceedings are commenced by the filing of a notice of motion, with annexures, with the registrar of the court.[136] The notice of motion must comply with a prescribed form and is addressed to the registrar. It must set out the relief sought and contain an address for service. It must also state the time within which the respondent must notify the applicant of his or her intention to oppose the application and the date on which the application will be heard if no such notification is given. This must be served on each party to whom notice is given by the sheriff. The notice of motion is accompanied by a founding affidavit setting out the facts upon which the applicant relies for the relief sought. This may be accompanied by various annexures, including other affidavits. It must be divided into consecutively numbered paragraphs and attested before a commissioner of oaths.

182. If the respondent wishes to oppose the application, he or she must file an answering affidavit within the time stated in the notice of motion that deals, paragraph by paragraph, with the applicant's allegations and provides the respondent's own version of the relevant facts. The applicant may deliver a replying affidavit in response. This may not include new matter or matter that should have been included in the founding affidavit but is intended to be a mere answer to the answering affidavit. The court has discretion to permit the filing of further affidavits by the parties.

183. The applicant, or failing him or her, the respondent, may then apply for a hearing date. At the hearing, legal argument is orally submitted to the court by the parties or their legal representatives.

184. Application procedure on notice is substantially similar in the Constitutional Court to that in the High Court.[137] However, the Chief Justice may direct that oral

135. Constitutional Court Rule 11(4).
136. *See* Uniform Rule 6, Form 2(a) Sch. 1, Uniform Rules.
137. *See* Constitutional Court Rules 11, 13 and Form 2, Sch. 1 Constitutional Court Rules.

evidence is not allowed, in which instance written argument may be called for, or the case may be dealt with on the basis of the information contained in the affidavits before the court. The court may also order that two or more cases, which involve the same or related questions, be argued together as one case.

185. Application proceedings take the same form in the Magistrates' Courts.[138] No provision is made for application procedure in Small Claims Courts.

10. Determination of the Trial Date

a. Obtaining a Trial Date

186. In High Court action proceedings, a trial or a hearing date may be requested immediately after the pleadings have closed. It is the prerogative of the plaintiff to apply for set down, but if he or she fails to do so within a certain time, the defendant may apply for a date. A notice requesting a trial date must be filed with the registrar of the court and notice that this has been done must be given to all other parties.[139] No uniform procedure exists, and each division of the High Court has its own rules as to how trial dates are allocated. The registrar compiles a list of trial dates that is usually published at least six weeks beforehand. Notice of the trial date is sent to all the parties by the registrar.

187. Magistrates' Courts Rule 22 provides that the plaintiff must deliver a notice of trial for a day approved by the clerk of the court after the close of pleadings. If the plaintiff does not do so within fifteen days, the defendant may do so or apply for dismissal of the action. Notice of the date must be given to other parties at least twenty days before the trial date.

b. Transfer of Actions

188. A party may apply to the High Court in which action was instituted for the matter to be transferred to another court.[140] The court must hear all the parties before making such an order and will only order removal if satisfied that the matter could more conveniently be heard at the new venue. The parties are also entitled to have a matter transferred to a Magistrate's Court. The consent of both parties is required and written application to a judge must be made before the commencement of the trial. The Magistrate's Court must have jurisdiction by consent or otherwise. A Magistrate's Court action in which the amount claimed exceeds a specified ceiling may be removed to the High Court having jurisdiction upon application by the defendant. Notice of the application must be given to the plaintiff before the date of hearing. The defendant must state his or her objections to having the matter heard before a Magistrate and

138. *See* Magistrates' Courts Rule 55.

139. Uniform Rule 29(2)(b) provides that a party who applied for a trial date must within ten days of notification to the registrar deliver a notice informing all other parties of the dates on which the matter is set down for trial. Rule 29 now contains a reference to both close of pleadings and notice of set down of trial.

140. *See* s. 27 of the Superior Courts Act 10 of 2013, Uniform Rule 39(22) and s. 50 of the Magistrates' Courts Act of 1944.

furnish such security as the court determines. If the defendant complies with these requirements, the action must be stayed. The plaintiff may then elect to remove the action or issue summons afresh in any division of the High Court having jurisdiction. If the plaintiff is successful in an action that has been removed, he or she may be awarded costs on an attorney-and-client scale, as the cost of litigation is higher in the High Court.

c. Offers to Settle

189. In the High Court, although an offer to settle made in terms of the Uniform Rules bears certain similarities to the common law procedure known as tender, the statutory procedure offers certain advantages.[141] A tender in terms of the common law must be unconditional, has no time limit within which it must be accepted, and if pleaded, renders the defendant liable for that amount even if a court finds him or her not liable, or liable for a lesser amount. Such an offer must be made directly to the plaintiff or his or her attorney and does not provide protection against a costs order unless pleaded. The statutory counterpart provides that a defendant may at any time make a written offer to settle the plaintiff's claim. The amount offered may comprise the whole claim or only a portion thereof. The offer must be signed by the defendant or his or her attorney and must indicate if it is unconditional (i.e., liability is admitted) or without prejudice (i.e., liability is denied). It must also indicate whether it is accompanied by an offer to pay all or only a part of the plaintiff's costs and whether it is by way of settlement of both claim and costs or of the claim only. If the defendant disclaims liability for the payment of costs, the reasons for such disclaimer must be given. An offer may be made not only to settle a monetary claim but also to perform an act, in which instance if the performance is not by the defendant personally, he or she must execute an irrevocable power of attorney authorizing the act. The plaintiff may accept the offer within fifteen days of receipt of notice of the offer by delivering a notice of acceptance. If the offer is not accepted within this period, it may thereafter only be accepted with the written consent of the defendant or the consent of the court. The defendant must comply with his or her offer within ten days of acceptance thereof. If he or she fails to do so, the plaintiff may apply for judgment in terms of the offer plus costs. Execution procedure can then be used to compel compliance with the judgment. The existence of an offer made without prejudice may not be disclosed to the court before judgment and a party who contravenes this provision, even if he or she is successful in the action, is liable to have costs awarded against him or her. The offer is disclosed to the court after judgment but before a costs order is made, as the fact that an offer was made is relevant to the apportionment of costs. If an offer that was rejected subsequently on judgment transpires to have been sufficient, the plaintiff is as a rule ordered to pay both parties' costs incurred from the date of offer. If the court awards a greater amount than that offered, the plaintiff will be awarded his or her full costs.

190. The position is similar in Magistrates' Courts.

191. Apart from these procedures, parties are always free to negotiate a settlement between themselves. If a compromise is reached that results in agreement, the matter

141. *See* Uniform Rule 34; Magistrates' Courts Rule 18.

is settled and if one of the parties subsequently attempts to proceed with the original action, the existence of a settlement can be pleaded. In the High Court, no statutory provisions deal with this form of settlement, and it is governed solely by the arrangements reached between the parties. In the Magistrates' Courts, provision is made for the recording of settlements reached between parties. This may be done either during the hearing of the action, if all parties are represented, or prior to the hearing by application on notice.

192. A court may be requested to make any settlement an order of court, in which instance it has the effect of a judgment by consent and is capable of immediate enforcement in the event of non-compliance. Alternatively, the court can merely record the terms of the settlement without entry of judgment. A statement of the terms of the settlement, signed by all the parties to the action, must be lodged with the court, and once the settlement has been recorded, all further proceedings are stayed. When the judgment has been recorded but not made a court order and the settlement provides for the future fulfilment of stated conditions that are not complied with, the party requiring compliance may apply for the entry of judgment in terms of the settlement within twelve months of non-compliance. Notice must be given to the other party setting out particulars of the breach. The court may dismiss the application, give judgment as specified in the terms of settlement, or set aside the settlement and give directions for further prosecution of the action.

d. Interim Payments

193. Provision exists in the High Court and Magistrates' Courts for the payment of interim damages in respect of actions for personal injuries or death.[142] These provisions were introduced to minimize the financial hardship suffered by a plaintiff or his or her next of kin occasioned by the delay in the finalization of litigation. A plaintiff may apply to court at any time after expiry of the period for the delivery of the notice of intention to defend for an order requiring the defendant to make an interim payment in respect of his or her medical costs, loss of income arising from his or her physical disability, or loss of income arising from the death of another person, usually a breadwinner. The supporting affidavit must set out the grounds for the application, the amount claimed and the documentary proof on which the plaintiff relies. The court must be satisfied that the defendant has admitted liability in writing or that a court has found the defendant liable but that damages have not yet been determined. In addition, it must be shown that the defendant is insured in respect of the claim or has the means at his or her disposal to make the payment. The court has a discretion as to the amount it awards, but it may not exceed a reasonable proportion of the damages the plaintiff is likely to recover, taking into account any contributory negligence, set off or counterclaim. The court may also prescribe the further conduct of the action and order an early trial date. The interim order must be paid in full, and its existence may not be disclosed to the trial court before judgment on quantum is given. The trial court may also order the plaintiff to repay all or part of the interim payment or vary or discharge the payment. A plaintiff may bring more than one application for an interim payment.

---

142. Uniform Rule 34A, Magistrates' Courts Rule 18A.

11. Trial

194. Trials do not take place in the Constitutional Court, as all proceedings are by way of application.

195. In High Court trials, a purely adversarial approach is followed with the judge serving as a passive and impartial observer of the proceedings. A judge is expected to carefully avoid any form of intervention that might create the impression he or she has prejudged the matter or is biased, and a judge should only intervene at the request of one of the parties. The parties themselves formulate the issues in dispute and determine what evidence they wish to present for the consideration of the court. The court may not itself require evidence to be led which the parties have chosen not to disclose and must make a finding on the available evidence. Although detailed provisions for the conduct of High Court trials are contained in the Uniform Rules,[143] these rules also provide that the court may at any time make any order regarding the conduct of a trial as seems fair and thereby vary any procedure contained in the rules. All proceedings must take place in open court unless the court directs otherwise due to special circumstances. The advocate for the party alleging such circumstances must provide brief reasons showing that it is in the interests of justice that the case be heard *in camera*. Parties and witnesses may use the South African language of their choice during proceedings. A sworn interpreter is used to translate evidence given in a language with which the court or one of the parties is not conversant. In the High Court, a party may appear in person or may be represented by an advocate or an attorney with an admission certificate.

196. On the date allocated for the hearing of the trial, the trial roll is called and the legal representatives appearing in the various trials set down for hearing on that day indicate which trials are ready to proceed. A court is then allocated to hear each trial that is proceeding. At the opening of the trial, either party may request a ruling from the court on the onus of adducing evidence. Such a ruling may thereafter be altered to prevent injustice. If the burden of proof is on the plaintiff, his or her advocate will address the court first and briefly outline the facts he or she intends to prove to establish the cause of action. The witnesses for the plaintiff are then sworn in and led and, after having given their evidence in chief, may be cross-examined and re-examined. If the defendant is of the opinion that a prima facie case has not been established by the plaintiff, he or she may address the court and apply for absolution from the instance at the close of the plaintiff's case. The plaintiff is entitled to reply. If absolution is not requested or not granted, the defendant may address the court, briefly setting out the facts he or she intends to prove, and thereafter proceed to the proof thereof. Defence witnesses are also subject to cross-examination and re-examination. After both parties have closed their cases, the plaintiff, and thereafter the defendant, may address the court. The plaintiff may reply to matters arising from the defendant's address. However, a court may, *mero motu* or on application by one of the parties, direct that proceedings be stayed if it appears that there is a question of law or fact that may be decided conveniently before evidence is led or separately from other questions.

197. Statutory provision is also made for instances when third parties or defendants to claims in reconvention who are not plaintiffs in the main action are involved. Such

143. Uniform Rule 39.

parties will usually give their opening address and lead evidence after the evidence of the plaintiff and defendant has been led but prior to the closing addresses of these parties, unless the court determines otherwise.

198. Generally, once a party has closed his or her case, he or she may not reopen it to lead further evidence. However, a court has a discretion to grant an application of a party for leave to reopen his or her case. Case law has laid down several general principles when considering such applications: the applicant must show that he or she displayed proper diligence in attempting to procure the evidence at the trial or that he or she did not lead the evidence he or she now wishes to adduce because he or she was taken by surprise and could not reasonably have known that it was relevant to the case. In addition, the evidence he or she wishes to lead must be material, but he or she need not show that it would be conclusive if believed. The court must also consider the prejudice to the other party (e.g., the difficulty of recalling witnesses). A case may be reopened at any time before judgment.

199. Because all Superior Courts are courts of record, a record must be made of all evidence, arguments, other proceedings (e.g., inspections *in loco* and demonstrations by witnesses) and judgments. The record is usually either taken down in shorthand or recorded, but is not transcribed unless the court so directs or at the request of a party on payment of the prescribed fees.

Provision is made in the rules for inspections *in loco* to afford the court the opportunity to see and note matters upon which there is no agreement.

200. The Act also makes provision for certain matters to be referred to a referee for investigation.[144] Matters that require extensive examination of documents or scientific, technical or local investigation that the court feels it cannot conveniently conduct, matters relating wholly or partially to accounts, and other matters arising in such proceedings may be referred for enquiry and report. The court may adopt the report either wholly or in part and with or without modifications; once adopted, the report will have effect of a finding by the court.

201. Either party may request a postponement of the trial before or on the day of the trial. The party must show good cause why he or she is not in a position to proceed, and the granting of a postponement lies in the court's discretion. The court will consider the prejudice to both parties before granting or refusing a postponement. It is usual for the responsible party to pay the wasted costs of a postponement. A postponement to lead further evidence may also be requested during the course of a trial. The applicant must show that such evidence is relevant and material and that it is not due to his or her fault that it is not immediately available.

202. If a defendant fails to appear at the trial, the plaintiff may request judgment without leading evidence if the claim is for a debt or liquidated demand. If the claim is unliquidated, he or she must lead evidence to prove it. When a plaintiff is in default at the trial, the defendant is entitled to an order granting absolution from the instance with costs but may lead evidence to satisfy the court that a final judgment should be granted in his or her favour.

203. The course of a trial in the Magistrates' Courts is similar to the procedure detailed above. However, parties to a Magistrate's Court action may also be represented by any attorney and by certain candidate attorneys.

---

144. Section 38 Superior Courts Act 10 of 2013.

204. Trial procedure in Small Claims Courts differs completely from that in other courts. The parties are unrepresented, and the commissioner proceeds inquisitorially to ascertain the relevant facts. The clerk of the court allocates a hearing date on which both parties must appear in person. Any South African language may be used by the parties and witnesses, and provision is made for an interpreter if required. All evidence must be given under oath. The usual rules of evidence and procedure do not apply in these courts, and a court may ascertain any relevant fact in such manner as it deems fit. Evidence may be presented in writing or orally. The presiding officer may question the parties and any witnesses at any stage of the proceedings, but the parties are not entitled to cross-question each other or witnesses unless the commissioner permits them to do so. The court may decide at any stage that sufficient evidence has been adduced on which a decision can be reached and can then order that no further evidence be led. A plaintiff may withdraw his or her action at any stage of the proceedings with the consent of the court and subject to such conditions as the court determines. If the defendant is in default at the trial, judgment may be given against him or her, while if the plaintiff is in default, the court may dismiss his or her claim. The court may also grant postponements when necessary. These courts are not courts of record, and only the judgment or order is recorded.

C. Judgment

1. Judgments of the Constitutional Court

205. The Constitution provides that a decision of the Constitutional Court is binding on all persons and all legislative, executive, and judicial organs of State. If this court finds that any law or provision thereof is inconsistent with the Constitution, it must declare such law or provision invalid to the extent of its inconsistency but may suspend the declaration of invalidity for any period and on any conditions to allow the competent authority to correct the defect. The relevant law or provision will then remain in force pending correction. Provision is also made that, if a law or provision is declared invalid, an order may be made limiting the retrospective effect of the declaration of invalidity. The same provisions apply should a court declare an executive or administrative act or conduct of an organ of State to be unconstitutional. The Constitutional Court must also confirm any order made by another court declaring national or provincial legislation invalid.[145] The Constitutional Court may make such costs orders as it deems just and equitable.[146]

2. Judgments of the Supreme Court of Appeal and the High Courts

a. Deliberation

206. In all Superior Courts, judgment is frequently not given immediately after the close of the parties' cases but reserved and given at a later stage. No time limit is set within which the judgment must be given. Judgment must be given in open court,

145. Section 167(5) Constitution of the Republic of South Africa, 1996.
146. Section 172 Constitution of the Republic of South Africa, 1996.

but it is not essential that the judge who heard the matter and prepared the judgment hand it down.

b. Different Kinds of Judgments

207. At the end of the trial, a judge will consider who bears the onus of proof and whether it has been discharged. If the onus is on the plaintiff and he or she has discharged it, the court will give judgment for the plaintiff; if not discharged, the court will grant absolution from the instance or, if the balance of probabilities favours the defendant, may grant judgment for him or her. If absolution is granted, the matter does not become res judicata, and the plaintiff may proceed afresh. If judgment for the defendant is given, the matter is res judicata, and the plaintiff may not institute a further action on the same grounds. Where the onus rests on the defendant and he or she fails to discharge it, judgment must be given for the plaintiff. If discharged, judgment for the defendant is given. The court has discretion to make any costs order it thinks necessary.

c. Formal Aspects of the Judgment

208. The only formality that must be complied with when judgment is given is the requirement that it must be delivered in open court.

d. Notice and Service

209. Although statutory provision is not made for notice of judgments to be given to parties, if proof of notice is required and the party or his or her legal representative was not present in court when judgment was handed down, the sheriff is usually requested to serve the order of court on the party concerned. The return of service will then be proof that the judgment came to the notice of that party.

e. Res Judicata

210. For a judgment to be accepted as res judicata, it must be a final judgment in which the court deals with the merits of the case. As seen above, the grant of absolution from the instance does not render a matter res judicata. A subsequent plea of res judicata will only be successful if the two actions take place between the same parties or their successors in title, concern the same subject matter and are founded on the same cause of complaint.

f. Interpretation and Rectification of Judgments

211. Once a judgment has been delivered, the judge becomes *functus officio* and, as a general rule, may not alter or vary the judgment. However, where a judgment is ambiguous, the general principles that apply to the interpretation of documents are used to construe it. If the actual order forming part of the judgment is clear, it cannot be extended or restricted by the contents of the judgment as a whole. The court may be approached to interpret its judgment but may not alter its substance or hear evidence to vary it. A judgment may be supplemented in certain restricted instances, such as accessory orders for costs or interest. A court is also competent to correct clerical errors in its judgments. If a court is requested by both parties to add something to an order, the court may make such agreement part of the court order. A court may also suspend execution of an order for a specified period. In certain circumstances, a party may request the court to set a judgment aside. The Uniform Rules provide that a court may, *mero motu* or at the request of a party, rescind a judgment or order erroneously sought or erroneously granted in the absence of any party affected thereby, or in which there is an ambiguity, patent error or omission, but only to the extent of such ambiguity, error or omission, or granted as a result of a mistake common to the parties.[147] In addition, at common law a judgment can be set aside if it was obtained by fraud involving the successful party or possibly if new documents come to light that, if they had been available at the trial, would have entitled the party claiming relief to judgment in his or her favour.

g. Penalty in Case of Non-compliance

212. A judgment becomes superannuated three years after the date on which it was pronounced, and a warrant of execution may not be issued after this period without the consent of the debtor or unless the court revives the judgment on notice to the debtor. If a party fails to comply with a court order, he or she is in contempt of court. This is a criminal offence, and he or she can be prosecuted by the State. However, civil contempt proceedings can also be instituted against him or her in the court that granted the order. Execution procedures, which are dealt with in paragraphs 310–315 are also available.

h. Judgments in Magistrates' Courts

213. The procedure in Magistrates' Courts is similar. However, these courts are specifically authorized to make a further order that is given against a successful party suspending wholly or in part the taking of further proceedings upon the judgment for a specified period pending arrangements by the unsuccessful party for the satisfaction of the judgment. Judgments cannot be set aside on common law grounds. It is statutorily provided that a judgment can be set aside if granted in the absence of a party or if void or obtained by fraud or mistake common to the parties. Patent errors can be corrected if no appeal is pending. Any judgment in respect of which no appeal lies (i.e., interlocutory orders that do not have the effect of a final judgment) can also be rescinded or varied.[148]

i. Judgments in Small Claims Courts

214. Small Claims Courts may give the same judgments as Magistrates' Courts, except that a costs order may only cover court and messengers' fees. Provision is also

147. Uniform Rule 42.
148. Section 36 Magistrates' Courts Act 32 of 1944.

made for a judgment to be set aside in similar instances to those in Magistrates' Courts, subject however to specific time limits.[149]

II. Provisional Proceedings

215. No proceedings whereby a provisional judgment is given exist in the Constitutional Court.

216. In the High Court and in Magistrates' Courts, a procedure known as provisional sentence is available in certain instances. The procedure is not available in Small Claims Courts. This procedure is derived from the Roman-Dutch *namptissement* and although the procedure is statutorily regulated,[150] Roman-Dutch principles are still referred to when the rules do not deal with a point. Provisional sentence provides a creditor whose claim is based on a liquid document with a summary but provisional judgment that entitles him or her to immediate execution, provided he or she gives the defendant security *de restituendo*. A court will only grant provisional sentence if the claim is based on a liquid document and if the plaintiff satisfies the court that the probabilities of success would be in his or her favour in the principal case.

217. A liquid document has been defined as a written instrument signed by the defendant or his or her agent showing an unconditional acknowledgement of indebtedness in a fixed amount of money. Examples of such documents are cheques, bills of exchange, promissory notes, acknowledgments of debt, and mortgage bonds.

218. Once the plaintiff has satisfied the court that the document is liquid and that *ex facie* the document the defendant is liable, the court must grant the order if the defendant fails to defend the matter. Where the defendant defends the matter, regard must be given to where the onus of proof lies. Although the question is the subject of debate and conflicting decisions, the plaintiff usually bears the onus in respect of defences relating to the liquidity of the document such as the following: the authenticity of the defendant or his or her agent's signature, the authority of the defendant's agent, fulfilment of any simple conditions and his or her entitlement to the claim evidenced by the liquid document. The defendant bears the onus in respect of all other issues – that is, defences outside the liquid document.

219. Proceedings are instituted by way of a provisional sentence summons, which is issued by the registrar and addressed to the sheriff, instructing him or her to inform the defendant to pay the amount of the claim or to appear personally or represented by counsel to admit or deny liability. If the defendant denies liability, he or she is called upon to file an affidavit setting forth the grounds of defence. The defendant must also be informed that if he or she fails to pay the amount or raise a defence, provisional sentence will be granted against him or her with costs, but that he or she is entitled to security *de restituendo* if he or she pays the amount. The summons must set out the cause of action with particularity and clarity, and a true copy of the liquid document on which it is based must be attached. The plaintiff must set the case down for hearing before midday two days before the hearing date and any affidavits the defendant wishes to file must also be delivered within this period. The plaintiff

149. Section 36 Small Claims Courts Act 61 of 1984.
150. Uniform Rule 8, Magistrates' Courts Rule 14A.

may reply to this affidavit, but a further affidavit by the defendant will only be allowed in exceptional circumstances. On the hearing date, the defendant may appear personally or duly represented. The court may hear oral evidence about the authenticity of the signature of the defendant or his or her agent or about the agent's authority, if these matters are in dispute. However, it does not have the power to order that oral evidence be led on other issues.

220. After considering the evidence, the court may grant or refuse provisional sentence or may even grant final judgment where the defendant has admitted liability, either at the hearing or prior thereto by filing an admission of liability with the registrar. The effect of the grant of provisional sentence is that the plaintiff is immediately entitled to payment or, failing that, to take out a writ of execution against the defendant's property. However, the plaintiff must on demand furnish the defendant with security *de restituendo*. The judgment is provisional in the sense that the defendant may enter into the principal case within two months by giving notice of his or her intention to do so, but only if he or she has satisfied the judgment debt and costs or if the plaintiff has failed to furnish security. If the defendant gives such notice, the summons is deemed to be a combined summons to which the defendant must deliver a plea within ten days. In default of a notice or plea, the judgment becomes final and the security given by the plaintiff lapses. If provisional sentence is refused by the court, it may order the defendant to file a plea within a stated time and make a costs order that seems just, and the usual trial procedure then continues. A provisional sentence judgment may be rescinded, but it is only appealable in certain circumstances.

221. The only other existing provisional proceeding is the interim interdict, where an interdict is granted for a specific period pending the outcome of a full hearing. This procedure is discussed in Part VIII (*see*, specifically, paragraph 295).

§2. Default Proceedings

I. High Court

222. The Uniform Rules make provision for judgments on confession and by default.[151] A defendant may at any time before judgment confess in whole or in part to the claim contained in the summons, unless it is for relief in terms of the Divorce Act 70 of 1979 or for nullity of marriage. This is generally known as consent to judgment and must be contained in a formal document, signed by the defendant personally with the signature either witnessed by his or her attorney or verified by affidavit. The confession, which must be complete and ready for judgment to be given on it, must be furnished to the plaintiff. The plaintiff may then, without notice to the defendant, apply through the registrar to a judge for judgment. The plaintiff may not add anything to a consent, and the defendant may not withdraw a consent. However, if there is any irregularity in the consent, it may be set aside.

223. A default judgment may be granted if the defendant is in default of delivery of his or her notice of intention to defend or his or her plea. When a defendant is in

151. Uniform Rule 31.

default of appearance, different procedures are followed depending on whether the claim is for a debt or liquidated amount or not. If the claim is for a debt or liquidated demand, the plaintiff may, without notice to the defendant, file a written application for judgment with the registrar. The registrar may grant or refuse judgment, in whole or in part. However, the registrar may not declare immovable property executable to the extent that this permits the sale in execution of a person's primary residence. He or she may also request oral or written submissions or require the matter to be set down for hearing in open court. If a party is dissatisfied with the registrar's decision, he or she may set the matter down for reconsideration by the court. Where the claim is unliquidated, notice need also not be given to the defendant. However, the matter is heard by a judge, not the registrar, and evidence must be led. Where the defendant is in default with his or her plea, it is necessary to serve a notice of bar on him or her calling on him or her to deliver a plea within five days. If the defendant fails to do so, notice of any application to court for default judgment must then be served on him or her. If the claim is liquidated, the court may grant judgment without hearing evidence, while if the claim is unliquidated, evidence must be led.

224. Default judgments may be set aside in terms of this rule in certain circumstances. A defendant must apply to the court for rescission, on notice to the plaintiff, within twenty days after he or she has knowledge of the judgment. He or she must furnish security to the plaintiff for payment of the costs of the default judgment and of the application. He or she must also show 'good cause' for the rescission. A reasonable explanation of his or her default must be given, his or her application must be bona fide and not merely intended to delay the plaintiff's claim, and a bona fide defence to the plaintiff's claim must also be shown. The court has discretion as to whether, and on what terms, it will set aside the default judgment. It should be noted that rescission of a judgment may now also take place with the plaintiff's consent in writing or where the judgment debt has been paid.[152]

II. Magistrates' Courts

225. Provision also exists in these courts for consent to judgment.[153] A consent form is endorsed on all summonses commencing action and this, or a similar form, may be signed by the defendant at any stage of proceedings. A defendant may consent for less than the amount claimed, in which case the action may proceed in respect of the balance of the claim. The consent is lodged with the clerk of the court. The plaintiff may obtain judgment by filing a request for judgment, accompanied by a copy of the letter of demand, if summons has not yet been issued, and the written consent to judgment, with the clerk of the court. The clerk may himself grant judgment unless the consent is contained in the defendant's plea.

152. Section 14 of the Courts of Law Amendment Act 7 of 2017 has amended the Superior Courts Act 10 of 2013 by inserting this clause section 23A.

153. Section 58 Magistrates' Courts Act 32 of 1944, Magistrates' Courts Rule 11 and s. 6 of Courts of Law Amendment Act 7 of 2017.

226. Default judgment is available,[154] and the procedure is substantially similar to that in the High Court. The only notable difference is that the clerk of the court may grant any judgment based on a liquidated claim, irrespective of whether the defendant is in default with his or her notice of intention to defend or his or her plea. However, requests for judgment based on unliquidated claims or credit agreements governed by the National Credit Act 34 of 2005, must be referred to the court. Such judgments may be set aside by applying to court within twenty days after the judgment has come to the applicant's knowledge, on notice to the other party. Good cause for the failure to enter appearance to defend or to plead, and the grounds of defence to the main action must be shown in the applicant's supporting affidavit. Security must also be furnished.

227. A Small Claims Court may grant judgment for a plaintiff if a defendant, after service of summons, either admits liability and consents to judgment in writing or fails to appear before the court on the trial date.[155] However, in all instances, the plaintiff must prove the defendant's liability and the amount of the claim to the satisfaction of the court. Such judgments may be rescinded provided that the application for set down is made within six weeks after the applicant had knowledge of the judgment.

§3. Ex Parte Proceedings

228. Ex parte proceedings are only instituted by way of a specific form of application procedure.[156] The procedure may be used in the following circumstances: where the applicant is the only person affected by the relief sought; where the relief is preliminary to the main proceedings and necessary to bring other interested parties before the court; where the procedure is prescribed by legislation; where notice to other parties would render the relief sought nugatory; where notice cannot be given to other parties due to the urgency of the matter; and in certain circumstances where the respondents are so numerous that it would be extremely difficult to notify them. Where an application is brought ex parte, the court requires the applicant to disclose fully all material facts that may affect its decision, even if such facts could prejudice the success of the application.

229. The application is commenced by notice of motion, which must comply with the prescribed form.[157] It is addressed to the registrar only, and no respondent is cited. A founding affidavit must set out the facts upon which the applicant relies for the relief sought. If the application is brought on an urgent basis, the court may dispense with the forms and service provided for in the rules.

230. Where the applicant is the only person affected by the relief sought, the court may immediately grant a final order. However, if the rights of other persons are involved, the court will issue a *rule nisi*, calling on the respondent or interested parties, to show cause on a stated day why the relief specified in the *rule nisi* should not be granted. Where the applicant has made out a case for the grant of immediate relief,

154. Magistrates' Courts Rule 12.
155. Section 35 Small Claims Courts Act 61 of 1984.
156. *See* Uniform Rule 6(4).
157. Form 2 Sch. 1 Uniform Rules.

the court will order that the *rule nisi* operate as an interim order until its confirmation or discharge on the return day. The court can specify parties on whom the *rule nisi* must be served, and parties affected by the rule may anticipate the return day on 24 hours' notice. The procedure in Magistrates' Courts is substantially similar.[158]

158. *See* Magistrates' Courts Rule 55(5)–(8).

Chapter 3. Review Proceedings

231. In most instances where a party is dissatisfied with the decision of a court, his or her objections necessitate the institution of either appeal or review proceedings. It is essential to determine which of the two procedures is apt in the given circumstances. In an appeal, the merits of the case are re-examined by a higher tribunal who decides on the correctness of the original decision and may reach a different decision. The court to which appeal is noted is limited to the information placed before the Court of First Instance. The objection is therefore to the result of the trial. Review proceedings are instituted if a party is dissatisfied with the method by which the result was obtained and is a limited rehearing at which the conduct of the original proceedings is scrutinized. It is thus often necessary to go beyond the record of the proceedings to determine the correctness of the procedure that was followed. For this reason, appeal and review procedures differ completely. Finally, unless exceptional circumstances exist, the Constitutional Court may only be approached on appeal or if a matter is referred to this court; both these procedures will be dealt with below.

§1. Appeal

232. A dissatisfied party does not always have a right to appeal a decision. No appeal whatsoever lies against the decision of a Small Claims Court. A party to an action in a Magistrate's Court has a statutory right of appeal to the High Court within whose jurisdictional area the Magistrate's Court is situated, and such appeals are heard by two judges of that court. Any further appeal lies to the Supreme Court of Appeal. When a matter has come before a High Court, either in first instance or on appeal, the court's leave is always necessary before an appeal can be noted. Where the original judgment was given by a single judge, the leave of that court – and, if refused, the leave of the Supreme Court of Appeal – must be obtained. The appeal will then be heard by a full court of the relevant High Court, unless the court granting leave to appeal is of the opinion that the matter requires the attention of the Supreme Court of Appeal. An appeal from the judgment of a full court lies to the Supreme Court of Appeal, if it grants leave to note appeal.[159] A further appeal may lie to the Constitutional Court.[160] Where an appeal has been noted, execution of the original judgment is suspended pending the outcome of the appeal, unless the court on application directs otherwise.

233. The procedure on appeal differs according to the court against whose decision appeal has been noted. In Magistrates' Courts, a written judgment is not usually given, and the first step is therefore to request reasons for judgment. This is done before appeal is noted to enable the party to assess his or her prospects on appeal. The judicial officer must furnish a written judgment showing the facts he or she found to be proved and his or her reasons for judgment. The appellant must then, within specified time limits, deliver a notice of appeal stating whether appeal is noted against

159. *See* s. 16 Superior Courts Act 10 of 2013.
160. Section 167 Constitution of the Republic of South Africa 1996.

the whole or only part of the judgment and stating his or her grounds of appeal, specifying the findings of fact or rulings of law appealed against. The judicial officer may then supplement his or her written judgment, if necessary, to deal with the grounds of appeal. The appeal is then set down for hearing, and the appeal court may confirm, vary or reverse the judgment. It may also remit the matter for further evidence, order the parties to give further evidence on appeal or take any other course to achieve a just, speedy, and inexpensive settlement of the case.[161]

234. An appeal against a decision by the High Court must always be preceded by a request for leave to appeal. This can be done orally at the time judgment is given or subsequently by filing an application for leave to appeal, which is heard by the judge who made the original order. If the leave of the Supreme Court of Appeal is necessary, the application is accompanied by a verifying affidavit, addressed to the Judge-President of the Supreme Court of Appeal. If leave is granted, a notice of appeal is filed, followed by the appeal record, which comprises all pleadings, documents, and evidence pertaining to the original trial and any subsequent appeals. A hearing date must then be requested and security furnished for the respondent's appeal costs. 'Heads of argument', which are concise statements of the main points to be argued on appeal and a list of authorities relied on, must be filed by both parties. The court hearing the appeal may confirm, amend or set aside the judgment that is the subject of the appeal. It may also receive further evidence or remit the case to the Court of First Instance for further hearing.[162]

§2. Review

235. The High Court has the power to review the proceedings of lower courts within its area. Proceedings of such courts may be reviewed on the grounds of absence of jurisdiction on the part of the court; interest in the cause, bias, malice or corruption on the part of the presiding officer; gross irregularity in the proceedings; the admission of inadmissible evidence; or the rejection of admissible evidence.[163]

236. The High Court also has inherent jurisdiction to review the proceedings of statutory bodies or domestic tribunals if they fail to conduct their proceedings in a fair and just manner. The grounds on which a court will intervene include misuse of power, *mala fides* or dishonesty, breach of the *audi alteram partem* rule, and gross unreasonableness. Various statutes also provide for a court review of decisions of statutory tribunals or officials.

237. Application procedure on notice is followed in review proceedings, with added provision for making the record available to all parties and provision that the applicant may amend or add to his or her application after receipt of the record.[164]

---

161. *See* in general in respect of appeals from Magistrates' Courts: Magistrates' Courts Rule 51, Uniform Rule 50 and s. 87 of the Magistrates' Courts Act 32 of 1944.
162. *See* in general ss 16–19 Superior Courts Act 10 of 2013, Supreme Court of Appeal Rules 6–10 and Uniform Rule 49.
163. Section 22 Superior Courts Act 10 of 2013; *see also* the Promotion of Administrative Justice Act 3 of 2000.
164. Uniform Rule 53.

§3. Appeals and Referrals to the Constitutional Court

I. Direct Appeals

238. A direct appeal from the High Court to the Constitutional Court is possible in constitutional matters when this is 'in the interests of justice'.[165]

239. In such circumstances, it is not necessary to obtain leave to appeal from the court that gave the order against which appeal is noted.

240. The appellant must lodge an application for leave to appeal with the Constitutional Court. This must contain the original decision and the grounds on which it is disputed, a concise statement of the constitutional issues raised in the decision, and any necessary supplementary information or argument. In direct appeals from a High Court, the appellant must also indicate whether he or she has applied for leave to appeal from any other court. This is to allow an applicant to also apply for leave to appeal to the next court in the appeal hierarchy, so that, should direct leave be refused, appeal proceedings can be instituted in that court. The respondent may reply, indicating whether he or she wishes to oppose the application for leave to appeal or wishes to lodge a cross-appeal. The Constitutional Court will then decide whether to grant leave, either summarily or after argument.[166]

241. Once leave to appeal has been granted, the appeal is prosecuted by filing an appeal record. The registrar thereafter requests written argument from both parties and, if the president so decides, the appeal may be dealt with on the basis of the written arguments only; otherwise, a hearing date is set at which the parties may present oral argument.[167]

II. Appeals from the Supreme Court of Appeal

242. An appeal on a constitutional issue from the Supreme Court of Appeal also requires the leave of the Constitutional Court. The procedure to obtain such leave is identical to that for applications from other courts, except that the appellant will not indicate whether he or she has applied for leave from any other court.[168]

III. Referrals to the Constitutional Court

243. The Supreme Court of Appeal and the High Court may make an order concerning the constitutional validity of parliamentary or provincial legislation or any conduct of the president. However, if a finding of invalidity is made, this has no force until confirmed by the Constitutional Court. All such orders must be referred to the

165. Section 167(6)(a) Constitution of the Republic of South Africa 1996.
166. Constitutional Court Rule 19.
167. Constitutional Court Rule 20.
168. Constitutional Court Rule 19.

Constitutional Court; pending its decision, the court that made the order of constitutional validity may grant a temporary interdict or other temporary relief.[169]

244. The registrar of the court that made the order must lodge a copy of this order with the registrar of the Constitutional Court. Persons and organs of State in favour of confirmation of this order may lodge applications for confirmation, while those against confirmation may file notices of appeal. In all cases, the Chief Justice provides directions on the further disposal of such matters.[170]

IV. Direct Access to the Constitutional Court

245. The Constitution provides that direct access to the Constitutional Court is possible where it is in the interest of justice to do so in respect of any matter over which this court has jurisdiction. The court has held that direct access is an extraordinary procedure and should be granted only in exceptional circumstances. Such circumstances will ordinarily exist only where the matter is urgent or otherwise of such public importance that the delay necessitated by use of the ordinary procedures will prejudice the public interest or the interests of justice. An application must be brought setting out the grounds on which it is contended that it is in the interests of justice that the order be granted, the nature of the relief sought and whether the matter can be dealt with without hearing oral evidence. The application must be served on all parties with a direct and substantial interest in the relief claimed. The Chief Justice then gives directions for the disposal of the matter.[171]

---

169. Section 172(2) Constitution of the Republic of South Africa 1996, s. 8(1)(a) Constitutional Court Complementary Act 13 of 1995.
170. Constitutional Court Rule 16.
171. Constitutional Court Rule 18.

Part V. Incidents

Chapter 1. Interlocutory Applications

246. An interlocutory application is incidental to pending proceedings; that is, it is a subordinate or accessory proceeding that is nevertheless distinct from the main proceedings. In the High Court, such applications may be brought on notice supported by such affidavits as the case may require.[172] 'Notice' in this context does not mean 'notice of motion' but merely a formal notice containing particulars of the parties, the relief requested and the hearing date. These applications need not be served by the sheriff, and service takes place on the party's attorney of record.[173] Further affidavits may be exchanged between the parties and the time limits relating to the times for exchanging answering and replying affidavits do not apply; however, a reasonable time must be allowed. An interlocutory order or ruling does not dispose of any issue in the main proceedings but has a merely procedural effect. It is therefore not a final judgment or order and is not open to appeal.[174] Such applications may also be brought in the Constitutional Court and in Magistrates' Courts.[175]

172. Uniform Rule 6(11).
173. Uniform Rule 4(1)(aA).
174. Section 17 Superior Courts Act 10 of 2013; s. 83 Magistrates' Courts Act 32 of 1944.
175. Constitutional Court Rule 29, Magistrates' Courts Rule 55(9).

Chapter 2. Withdrawal and Discontinuance of Action

§1. Withdrawal

247. In the Constitutional Court, a case may be withdrawn at any stage of the proceedings if all the parties lodge a written agreement to this effect with the registrar. The agreement must specify the terms relating to the payment of costs and the payment of any fees due to the registrar. The registrar then enters the withdrawal if directed to do so by the Chief Justice.[176]

248. In the Supreme Court of Appeal, an appellant or cross-appellant may withdraw his or her appeal. The stage at which this may be done is not specified. Provision is also made that if the appellant fails to lodge the record of proceedings within the specified time without having obtained an extension of time from the respondent, he or she is deemed to have withdrawn the appeal.[177]

249. In the High Court, a person who has instituted proceedings may withdraw them at any time before the matter is set down for hearing. Thereafter, the consent of the parties or leave of the court is required.[178] A notice of withdrawal is invalid without such consent or leave. The court has a discretion to grant leave to withdraw but will not usually force a person to proceed against his or her will. If a notice of withdrawal does not include an offer to pay costs, the other party may apply to court on notice for a costs order.

250. In the Magistrates' Courts, a summons may be withdrawn by merely notifying the clerk of the court, if the summons has not yet been served or no appearance to defend has been entered. In all other circumstances, a notice of withdrawal must be served on all parties, and if a consent to pay costs is not included in the notice, the other party may apply to the court for a costs order.[179]

§2. Discontinuance

251. No provision is made for discontinuance or postponements in the rules of the Constitutional Court. However, the court may give directions in matters of practice and procedure and may no doubt allow postponements in the exercise of this power.

252. In the High Court, parties may agree to postpone a matter.[180] If one of the parties seeks a postponement that is not agreed to by the other, the court must be approached on notice for the grant of a postponement. Good cause must be shown, and the court will take into account the prejudice that the grant or refusal of postponement will occasion to all parties. The costs incurred by the postponement are usually borne

---

176. Constitutional Court Rule 27.
177. Supreme Court of Appeal Rule 8(3).
178. Uniform Rule 41(1).
179. Magistrates' Courts Rule 27(1)–(3).
180. Uniform Rule 41(3).

by the party making the request. When a postponement is requested during the course of a trial for the purpose of leading new evidence, the applicant must show that the evidence is relevant and available, and that it was not due to his or her fault that the evidence was not available earlier.

253. Magistrates' Courts proceedings may be adjourned or postponed by consent of the parties or by the court, on application or *mero motu*. The court may make an order concerning costs of the postponement if the parties do not reach agreement.[181]

181. Magistrates' Courts Rule 31.

Chapter 3. Challenge of Judges

254. The Constitution gives every person the right to have disputes that can be resolved by the application of law decided before a court or, where appropriate, another independent and impartial forum.[182] All judicial officers, in the oath taken before commencing their functions, swear to 'administer justice to all persons alike without fear, favour or prejudice'.[183] When it is felt that an impartial decision will not be given by a specific judicial officer assigned to hear a matter, the common law has always acknowledged the right of a party to request that the officer concerned should recuse himself or herself. The Constitution now confirms this right. An objective test as to the likelihood of bias applies, and the applicant for recusal must prove reasonable cause.

255. The grounds on which an application may be brought are the following: interest in the cause, whether direct or indirect; close relationship or friendship with a party or possibly one of the legal representatives; colleagues attached to the same bench when one is a litigant and the other is acting as a judicial officer; clear proof of enmity or hostility toward a party; prior professional interest as legal representative of one of the parties by the judicial officer; expressions of opinions indicative of bias in connection with the case in question; and a situation in which the judicial officer is a material witness.

256. The procedure to be followed when objecting is known as the *exceptio suspecti judicis*. The objection is usually made *in limine* but may be raised later if the facts come to light at a later stage. The objection may be taken by either party and is usually heard by the judicial officer concerned. If the judicial officer recuses himself or herself, he or she becomes *functus officio* and may take no further part in the case. The existing proceedings become a nullity and the matter must be reheard. An appeal may be noted against the refusal of a judicial officer to recuse himself or herself. Some of the grounds on which refusal may be requested are also grounds for requesting review of the proceedings of a lower court.[184]

182. Section 34 Constitution of the Republic of South Africa 1996.
183. Schedule 2 s. 6(1), Constitution of the Republic of South Africa 1996; s. 9(2) Magistrates' Courts Act 32 of 1944; s. 9(6) Small Claims Courts Act 61 of 1984.
184. *See* para. 235.

Part VI. Legal Aid and Legal Costs

Chapter 1. Legal Aid

257. State-funded legal aid is provided by the Legal Aid Board, an autonomous body regulated by the Legal Aid South Africa Act 39 of 2014. The board's stated mission is to make available legal aid and legal advice, provide legal representation at State expense, and provide education and information regarding legal rights and obligations. The Act sets out the composition of the board, which consists of a Judge of the Supreme Court, the Director-General: Justice and Constitutional Development, the chief executive officer and another three employees of the board, and eight other members who have various business and legal skills. The head office of the board is situated in Johannesburg, with justice centres, High Court units, and satellite offices situated throughout the country.

258. The Act provides that the board is obliged to provide legal representation at State expense as envisaged in the Constitution where substantial injustice would otherwise result. In criminal matters, a court must take into account the personal circumstances of the person concerned and the nature and gravity of the charge. The Act is silent on the criteria to be applied in civil cases. In general, the Act gives the board a wide discretion by merely providing that it has the authority to fix the conditions subject to which legal aid is rendered. The directives of the board are contained in the Legal Aid Manual[185] and consist of rules made in terms of the Act. The board employs a number of legal practitioners who operate as justice centres and provide legal assistance. In other instances, it refers indigent persons to practitioners in private practice who are prepared to act at a reduced tariff of fees. Recipients of legal aid are allowed to deal with an attorney of their choice provided he or she is willing to act at the set tariff.

259. The current manual provides that, in civil matters, the board must be satisfied that there are merits in the case, and that there is a reasonable prospect of success and recovery. In line with the requirements placed on it by the Constitution, the Legal Aid Board has identified certain priorities for the rendering of assistance. These are to provide legal aid to: children in civil matters affecting them where substantial injustice would otherwise result; children in conflict with the law; every detained person (including sentenced prisoners); every person accused of a crime; those who wish to appeal or review a decision of a court in a higher court; women, particularly in divorces, maintenance and domestic violence cases; and the landless, especially with regard to evictions. An applicant for legal aid may appeal to the director

185. Available at www.legal-aid.co.za.

and thereafter to the Chairman of the Board regarding the refusal of legal aid. Decisions on the provision of legal aid in criminal matters may be subject to review by the High Court after internal appeals have been exhausted.

260. In criminal cases, legal aid is available to all indigent persons who are physically resident in South Africa. In civil cases, legal aid is available to all indigent people who are physically resident in South Africa and are citizens or permanent residents of the country. In exceptional circumstances, the director may grant legal aid in a matter which is justiciable in a South African court even though the applicant does not meet the residence requirement. The 'physical residence' requirement does not apply to asylum seekers and the Hague Convention. The Act contains no definition of the term 'indigent'; it merely states that a person seeking legal aid bears the onus of showing that he or she is unable to afford the cost of legal representation, has made full disclosure of all relevant facts, and has a lifestyle that is consistent with the alleged inability. Currently, a means test that takes into account the total financial situation of the applicant and spouse is applied to determine whether a person qualifies for legal aid. The income and assets of the applicant, and his or her spouse where applicable, are considered and a calculated income determined, which may not exceed a specified amount. This amount is revised periodically. Depending on his or her calculated income, an applicant may be required to make an initial contribution to the board's costs. Any rights to costs to which an applicant becomes entitled are deemed to have been ceded to the board. When an applicant becomes entitled to any financial benefit as a result of a settlement or a judgment during any stage after legal aid was granted, a percentage of this benefit must be deducted and paid to the board.

261. The Constitution has placed a heavy burden on the board as it provides that detained persons, including sentenced prisoners, and accused persons, are entitled to be provided with the services of a legal practitioner at State expense if substantial prejudice would otherwise result. Although this is only relevant in criminal matters, it has had the effect that less funds are available to assist civil litigants. For this reason, the board has begun to create justice centres staffed by their own employees and also cooperates with legal aid clinics attached to various universities to provide more cost-effective legal services. In addition, a number of advice and legal information centres are administered by various non-governmental organizations; in an effort to make these services more accessible and standardize their quality, the board also has cooperation agreements with some of these centres.

Chapter 2. Legal Costs

262. The purpose of an order for costs is to recompense a successful litigant for the expenses he or she incurred because he or she was obliged to institute or defend legal proceedings. Two types of costs order can be distinguished. The usual costs order a court will make is for party-and-party costs. This concept covers those costs incurred by a party to legal proceedings that the court orders the other party to pay to him or her. It does not cover all costs which the party might have incurred, but only such costs as were incurred in the actual litigation and which are allowed by the taxing master. Generally, costs incurred before the issue of summons are not considered party-and-party costs. The other type of costs order is known as attorney-and-client costs. A client's liability to pay such costs arises from his or her contractual relationship with an attorney and is unrelated to the outcome of the legal proceedings; payment is not dependent on any costs order. These costs include remuneration for all professional services rendered and all expenses incurred by the attorney in execution of his or her client's instructions. Such orders are not granted by a court unless special circumstances exist. A court can also order each party to pay its own costs.

263. When considering the award of costs, the basic rule is that such awards are in the discretion of the court. This judicial discretion requires the court to consider the circumstances of the case, the conduct of the parties and any other issues that might have a bearing on the award and then to make a fair decision. As a general principle, costs follow the event, and a successful party is awarded his or her party-and-party costs. To determine who is the successful party, a court considers the substance of the judgment and not merely its form. The court may also, in the exercise of its discretion, deprive the successful party of his or her costs having regard to the possibility of excessive demands by the party, the conduct of the litigation, the use of unnecessary steps or wrong procedures, and misconduct. Generally, separate issues carry their own costs, and a defendant who has been successful on a distinct issue wholly unconnected with the issue on which the plaintiff succeeded is entitled to costs in respect of that issue. The general rule that costs are awarded to the successful party also applies to costs on appeal. However, where a trial court has exercised a discretion and deprived a successful party of his or her costs in that court, an appeal court will not readily interfere. An attorney-and-client costs order will usually be granted against a party if he or she was guilty of dishonesty or fraud in the conduct of the litigation; if his or her motives were vexatious, reckless or malicious; or if he or she was guilty of serious misconduct in the course of the proceedings. Statutory provision is also made for such an award against a party who unreasonably instituted or defended summary judgment proceedings or who, without justification, requested transfer of an action from a Magistrate's Court to the High Court. When a person litigates in a representative capacity, usually as executor, trustee or legal representative, a court may make an order of costs *de bonis propriis* – that is, the person in the fiduciary position must pay costs from his or her own pocket – if such person was guilty of seriously improper or unreasonable conduct or absence of bona fides. In the Constitutional Court, it has been held that litigants should not be deterred from approaching the court by the threat of an adverse costs order, and that if the issues raised are important and controversial and the proceedings lead to a resolution of these issues, the applicant should not be penalized by an adverse costs order.

264. Before an award of costs can be enforced, it must be taxed by a court official. In the High Court a taxing master performs this function, while in Magistrates' Courts it is performed by the clerk of the court. The Uniform Rules aim to afford the party who has been awarded an order for costs full indemnity for all costs reasonably incurred by him or her in relation to his or her claim or defence and to ensure that all such costs shall be borne by the party against whom the order was made. Towards that end, the taxing master shall allow all such costs and expenses as appear to have been necessary or proper for the attainment of justice or for defending the rights of any party. However, costs that have been incurred or increased through over-caution, negligence or mistake, by payment of special fees to advocates, or in special charges and expenses to witnesses or other unusual expenses are not allowed.[186] A bill of costs is drawn up in accordance with the statutory tariff of fees applicable in the court concerned, and the taxing master has a discretion to decide what fees and expenses he or she considers to have been necessary. The decision of a taxing master or clerk of the court may be taken on review to the court concerned.[187] Taxation is not a prerequisite for the liability of a client to pay costs to his or her attorney.

265. Different types of costs order may be encountered when interim orders are made or when proceedings are postponed or adjourned. The rules do not make specific provision for costs occasioned by a postponement, but it is accepted that postponements should be granted unless the other party will suffer prejudice that cannot be met by a costs order. Three types of costs are relevant in such circumstances. Costs of postponement are the costs of the application for postponement. If a litigant is not responsible for the postponement, he or she is not generally ordered to pay the costs thereof. Costs of the day are the costs caused by the postponement and are usually paid by the applicant for a postponement. Wasted costs are additional costs resulting from a postponement and are awarded against the party responsible for the postponement. Where a litigant withdraws or abandons proceedings, he or she frequently includes an offer to pay costs in his or her notice and, if he or she fails to do so, a costs order can be sought. Where a matter is struck from the roll, the responsible party will usually be liable for costs. The court can also make orders for costs in respect of interim applications or objections. Apart from making a costs order against one of the parties, a court can reserve the costs of the proceedings for later decision or order that costs are in the cause (i.e., that the party who is ultimately successful will be entitled to those costs). A court has a discretion to stay proceedings where the costs of previous proceedings have remained unpaid, if the further proceedings cover substantially the same ground and have been brought vexatiously.

266. The general principles governing costs orders do not always apply where certain types of litigants are concerned. The State and the government are legal *personae*, and costs can be awarded against them. However, special rules apply where statutory and quasi-judicial bodies and public officers are concerned. A court will not award costs against such a party if his or her action, though mistaken, was bona fide; on the same basis, a court will not make a costs order against another party in favour of such

186. Uniform Rule 70(3).

187. Uniform Rule 48, s. 81 Magistrates' Courts Act 32 of 1944.

bodies and officers if that party acted bona fide and on reasonable grounds. It follows that in such instances a court will frequently make no order as to costs, unless the body or officer actively opposes proceedings and his or her motive is not merely to assist the court. In litigation concerning deceased estates, the costs are frequently ordered to come out of the estate. The taxed costs of a sequestration must also be borne by the free residue of the estate. Costs orders are also not usually made against unsuccessful pauper plaintiffs.

267. The common law provides that a plaintiff who is a *peregrinus* of South Africa (i.e., neither domiciled nor resident in the country) may be required to furnish security for the costs of litigation he or she institutes. An *incola* plaintiff is not required to do so, and this is statutorily confirmed in respect of plaintiffs in High Court litigation residing anywhere in South Africa.[188] A *peregrinus* who institutes a claim in reconvention should also furnish security for costs. In Magistrates' Courts, security may be demanded from a plaintiff, but the rules are silent as to when this may be ordered, and it appears that the discretion lies with the court as to whether a defendant is entitled to demand security.[189] A court has a discretion in regard to the furnishing of security but exercises it only in exceptional circumstances. A litigant who institutes vexatious litigation can also be required to furnish security, as can a plaintiff company where there is reason to believe that it will not be able to pay costs. Security is not furnished automatically but must be requested by the defendant. If a defendant wishes the plaintiff to provide security, he or she must deliver a notice setting forth the grounds on which security is claimed and the amount demanded, as soon as practicable after the commencement of proceedings. If the party from whom security is demanded contests his or her liability, an application must be made for the court to decide on the matter; if only the amount demanded is contested, this is determined by the registrar. If security is not given within a reasonable time, the court may dismiss the proceedings, strike out pleadings filed by the party in default or make any other order it thinks appropriate.

268. In Small Claims Courts, the only costs that may be awarded are court fees and the fees and travelling expenses of the messenger of the court.

188. Section 25 Superior Courts Act 10 of 2013.
189. Magistrates' Courts Rule 62(1).

Part VII. Evidence

269. The primary statute governing evidence in all civil proceedings, other than those in Small Claims Courts, is the Civil Proceedings Evidence Act 25 of 1965. However, large portions of the law of evidence are common law, based on the English law of evidence, as this Act contains a residuary section providing that, in cases not provided for in the Act or other laws, the law of evidence, including the law relating to the competency, compellability, examination and cross-examination of witnesses, which was in force on 30 May 1961 shall apply. Various provincial statutes, all containing residuary clauses incorporating English law for matters not specifically covered, were in force on that date. The effect is that, to a large extent, the English law of evidence as of that date applies in South Africa, except where amended by South African legislation. The English statute law in force when English law was introduced to the various provinces, but not subsequent amendments thereto, applies in South Africa. In addition, amendments to English law brought about by judicial decisions during the period between the introduction of English law and 30 May 1961 also apply. English decisions after 1961 are not binding on South African courts but do have persuasive value.

Chapter 1. Burden of Proof

270. The burden or onus of proof determines the result if, at the end of the trial, the evidence is inconclusive and the court cannot decide on a factual issue. In such an instance, the party bearing the burden for the particular issue has then failed to establish his or her claim or defence. The burden of proof is a matter of substantive law and is determined by the pleadings. It must be distinguished from the evidentiary burden of rebutting the opponent's case. The burden of proof is fixed at the commencement of a trial when the issues are determined and does not shift during the course of the trial. The evidentiary burden, on the contrary, shifts during the trial as each side leads evidence. Separate burdens of proof may exist in relation to different facts in issue, and the onus will not always rest on the same party. In certain circumstances, the burden of discharging a particular issue may not arise until another has been discharged. In an appeal on a factual issue, there is a presumption that the trial judge was correct. It can thus be said that, in the absence of special circumstances, the burden rests on the appellant as the appeal court will only reverse the decision if convinced that the trial court was wrong. As a general rule, the party bearing the evidentiary burden must adduce evidence first. The most important principles governing the determination of the burden of proof are the following: the fundamental rule is that he or she who asserts must prove, and it follows that the plaintiff must bear the onus. Where, however, the defendant makes an allegation that is denied by the plaintiff, the burden rests on the defendant to prove that issue. The burden also rests on the defendant with regard to any special defence (confession and avoidance) he or she raises. While a presumption of fact does not affect the burden of proof but merely places an evidentiary burden on the party against whom it operates, a presumption of law often places the burden of proof on such party. If a party has particular knowledge of a fact in issue, this does not place the burden of proving that fact on him or her. Statutory provisions can also specify, expressly or by implication, where the burden of proof rests. Judicial notice – in which a court takes into account a fact that has not been proved in evidence – does not affect the burden of proof but obviates the necessity of furnishing evidence on the point.

Chapter 2. Admissibility of Evidence

271. The basic rule is that to be admissible, evidence must be relevant. Evidence is relevant if the facts testified to tend, by themselves or in conjunction with other facts, to prove or disprove the facts in issue. To be legally relevant, evidence must be sufficiently relevant to warrant being received in the circumstances of the specific case. The value of the evidence is thus considered: if it has sufficient probative force to outweigh any disadvantages attached to admitting it, it is relevant; if the disadvantages outweigh its probative force, it is legally irrelevant. Evidence can be relevant either as facts in issue (*facta probanda*) or as facts relevant to the facts in issue (*facta probantia*). The former are the facts legally required to prove the claim or defence in dispute, while the latter are facts that tend to prove or disprove the existence of the facts in issue.

272. Both the rules derived from the English law of evidence, and South African legislation tends to approach the question of what evidence is admissible in negative terms, by emphasizing what is excluded rather than what is allowed. The following are some of the categories of evidence that are usually inadmissible.

273. The Constitution provides that evidence obtained in a manner that violates any right in the Bill of Rights must be excluded if its admission would make the trial unfair or be detrimental to the administration of justice.

274. The character of the parties and witnesses in civil trials is seldom relevant except in actions for defamation, seduction, and the like.

275. Similar fact evidence is admissible only if its probative value is strong enough to warrant its reception in the interests of justice, and its admission will not operate unfairly against other parties.

276. Opinion evidence is usually inadmissible because only the witness's observations are considered relevant, not the inferences he or she drew from such observations. However, expert opinion is admissible if relevant and if the expert is qualified – that is, if his or her skill, training or experience can materially assist the court on matters of which the court does not have the necessary knowledge.[190]

277. Admissions are admissible if made freely and voluntarily, unless made for the purpose of settlement in which case they are privileged. The Act also deals with admissions and provides that a fact admitted in the pleadings need not be proved and cannot be rebutted. The admission can, however, be withdrawn by amending the pleadings provided that a reasonable explanation is given that a bona fide error was made, and that the other party does not suffer prejudice that cannot be remedied by a costs order.[191]

278. Hearsay evidence is statutorily regulated.[192] It is defined as evidence, whether oral or in writing, the probative value of which depends on the credibility of any person other than the person giving evidence. It is inadmissible unless each party against whom the evidence is to be adduced agrees to its admission; when the person

190. The procedure for giving notice of expert evidence that will be presented at the trial is dealt with in para. 175. If proper notice is not given, such evidence will usually be inadmissible.

191. Section 15 Civil Proceedings Evidence Act 25 of 1965.

192. Section 3 Law of Evidence Amendment Act 45 of 1988.

on whose credibility the probative value of the evidence depends gives evidence; or where the court is of the opinion that it is in the interests of justice that the evidence be admitted. To determine the final circumstance, the court must have regard to the nature of the proceedings, the nature of the evidence, the purpose for which the evidence is tendered, the probative value of the evidence, the reason why the evidence is not being given by the person on whose credibility its probative value depends, any prejudice to a party by the admission of such evidence and any other factor that the court feels should be taken into account. Hearsay evidence may also be admitted provisionally if the court is informed that the person upon whose credibility the probative value of the evidence depends will testify. If he or she does not do so, the evidence is disregarded unless it qualifies in terms of one of the above exceptions.

279. Documentary hearsay evidence is also dealt with in the Act, which provides that the contents of a document are admissible in specific circumstances as proof of a particular fact.[193] The person who draws up the document must have personal knowledge of the particulars in it or must perform this activity in the execution of his or her duty to record information received from other people. This person is also required to testify in court unless he or she is deceased, unable to testify, or abroad and it is not practical for him or her to be present in court. The court may also admit documentary evidence even though the person who drew up the document does not testify, if doing so would prevent extraordinary delays and costs. Where a juridical act is contained in a document, extrinsic evidence of its terms is usually not admissible. Thus, when a transaction has been reduced to writing, no evidence may be given to alter, add to or contradict its terms.

280. Evidence that would otherwise be admissible may not be disclosed if privilege is successfully claimed. Private privilege, where the interests of an individual are protected, must be claimed by the witness concerned in response to the specific question, as the existence of the privilege does not exempt him or her from testifying. Various forms of private privilege exist. All communications made in confidence between a legal adviser, acting in his or her professional capacity, and his or her client, with a view to obtaining legal advice or to litigation, are privileged, and this privilege may be waived only by the client. Statements made without prejudice in a bona fide attempt to settle a dispute also enjoy privilege. The Act provides that a spouse may claim privilege in respect of communications made by the other spouse during the marriage. The privilege also applies to communications made during a marriage or putative marriage that has been dissolved or annulled, a customary marriage or union, and a marriage concluded under a system of religious law.[194]A witness may not claim privilege on the ground that the answering of a question may establish that he or she owes a debt or is subject to a civil suit.[195]

281. Public privilege, which protects the interests of the community as a whole, is usually claimed by a State organ or an official. At common law, the court will itself decide whether a claim of privilege should be upheld after scrutinizing the document concerned. Although the Constitution provides that everyone has the right of access to any information held by the State, national legislation enacted to give effect to this

193. Section 34 Civil Proceedings Evidence Act 25 of 1965.
194. Section 10, 10A Civil Proceedings Evidence Act 25 of 1965.
195. Section 14 Civil Proceedings Evidence Act 25 of 1965.

right places limits on access that might prejudice State security, defence or international relations.[196]

282. The Act also contains various provisions dealing with the admissibility of evidence.[197] For the purpose of rebutting a presumption of paternity, a spouse may give evidence that the spouses had no sexual intercourse during the period of conception. A comparison of a disputed handwriting with a writing proved to be genuine may be made by witnesses and submitted as evidence. Any law, government notice or other matter published in the Government Gazette is, on mere production of a copy of the Gazette, evidence of the contents of such law or other matter. A document purporting to bear the signature of a person holding public office and bearing the stamp of his or her office is, on mere production, prima facie proof that such person signed the document. A person who has called a witness may prove that the witness made an earlier statement that is inconsistent with his or her evidence.

§1. Competence of Witnesses

283. The Act provides that, save as otherwise provided by legislation or the common law, every person is competent and compellable to give evidence in civil proceedings.[198] The competence of a witness is an issue for the court to decide, and the parties cannot themselves agree to admit the evidence of an incompetent witness. The Act excludes persons appearing or proved to be afflicted with idiocy, lunacy or insanity or suffering from imbecility of mind due to intoxication or otherwise, whereby they are deprived of the proper use of reason.[199] The latter phrase is strictly interpreted so that feeble-minded persons may be competent to testify provided they are not deprived of the 'proper use of reason' in respect of the facts on which they give evidence. If a witness becomes incompetent during the course of a trial, evidence given before this occurred will stand insofar as it is not disputed by the other party. One spouse may testify for or against the other spouse. Children are not barred as witnesses and no specific age limit exists, but their testimony must be carefully scrutinized. The presiding officer may not testify in a trial and other judicial officers, although technically competent, are discouraged from doing so. Certain witnesses, although competent, cannot be compelled to give evidence. The president, heads of State and diplomatic representatives enjoy immunity, and parliamentary officials enjoy immunity while performing parliamentary functions. A judge can be subpoenaed to give evidence only with the leave of the court.

196. Section 32(1) Constitution of the Republic of South Africa 1996; s. 41 Promotion of Access to Information Act 2 of 2000.
197. Sections 3–7 Civil Proceedings Evidence Act 25 of 1965.
198. Section 8 Civil Proceedings Evidence Act 25 of 1965.
199. Section 9 Civil Proceedings Evidence Act 25 of 1965.

Chapter 3. Administration of Evidence

§1. Viva Voce Evidence

284. A party to a civil action cannot be compelled to give evidence, but failure to do so may lead the court to make an adverse inference. A witness may be subpoenaed to attend a trial and, if required to produce documents, should be informed of this in the subpoena. A witness who fails to attend court or produce documents after being served with a subpoena, or who refuses to answer questions during the trial, may be arrested, kept in prison to secure his or her attendance at the trial, and sentenced to a fine or imprisonment.[200] If the burden of proof rests on the plaintiff, he or she will lead his or her evidence first and thereafter close his or her case, after which the defendant leads evidence. Third parties adduce their evidence after the plaintiff and defendant.

285. Generally, evidence must be given viva voce under oath in open court. The side calling a witness first presents his or her examination-in-chief. Leading questions may not be put except in respect of introductory or non-disputed matters. The questioner may not impeach the credibility of his or her own witness. This means that he or she may not cross-examine the witness (unless the witness has been declared hostile), but he or she may dispute the witness's version of the facts by calling other witnesses to contradict him or her and also prove previous inconsistent statements. Cross-examination may be conducted by all other parties. In contrast with examination-in-chief, leading questions may be put at this stage, and questions may be put that are relevant only to credibility. Generally, inadmissible evidence may not be put to or elicited from the witness. In certain circumstances, inadmissible evidence will become admissible if the other party agrees or fails to object to it. Re-examination by the side who called the witness may take place but must be confined to matters arising from cross-examination. The court may ask questions at any stage of the proceedings but should confine any longer examination until after re-examination. The purpose of such questions should be to clarify the issues, and the court should remain impartial. A witness may refresh his or her memory from notes provided they are authentic – that is, made by him or her or on his or her instructions, made when the events were still fresh in memory, and provided he or she is prepared to waive any privilege he or she could otherwise claim in respect of them.

§2. Affidavit Evidence

286. In certain circumstances, evidence need not be presented orally. The court may, in its discretion, allow evidence to be given on affidavit if it is of a formal nature or if it would be extremely difficult or expensive for the witness to attend court. On application, a court may also order that the evidence of a witness be taken on commission or by interrogatories. In the latter case, specific questions are formulated which are

200. Section 35 Superior Courts Act 10 of 2013.

put to the witness by the commissioner, while in the former case evidence is given generally. The procedure is regulated statutorily.[201] Where evidence is to be given on commission, the witness is subpoenaed to appear before a commissioner, and his or her evidence is taken orally in the presence of the parties and their legal representatives. The evidence is recorded and sent to the registrar of the court concerned, where it becomes part of the record of the case. A commissioner may not decide on the admissibility of the evidence tendered, but must note any objections, which will be decided by the court hearing the matter. Evidence taken in the form of interrogatories is also taken by a commissioner, who puts duly framed questions to the witness and records his or her answers, which are then transmitted to the registrar of the court concerned.

§3. Real Evidence and Inspections

287. Real evidence is presented when an object such as a fingerprint or an item of clothing is shown to the court. It is usually adduced through a witness who gives evidence about the object to show its relevance. An expert witness can also be called to explain the object. Another form of real evidence is the scene of an event or an object that cannot be brought to court; these types of evidence may be viewed by the court during an inspection *in loco*. The decision to hold such an inspection rests in the discretion of the court, and the inspection should take place in the presence of the parties.

§4. Documentary Evidence

288. Documentary evidence includes everything that contains written or pictorial proof of something. Affidavits are viewed as documentary evidence. A distinction is made between public and private documents.

289. A public document is one drawn up by a public official in the execution of a public duty that is intended for public use and to which the public has access. Such documents may be tendered as testimony as an exception to the hearsay rule; they need not be identified or authenticated, and secondary evidence of their contents is admissible. A copy of such a document, certified as true by the official in whose custody it is kept, is admissible as evidence.

290. The pretrial procedures of discovery, inspection, and production are used to ascertain the existence of private documents that might have a bearing on the case.[202] If a document has not been discovered or admitted, it must be authenticated. This may be done by the author, executor or signatory, a person who signed the document as witness, a person who can identify the signature, or someone who has lawful control of the document. Documents that are more than twenty years old are presumed authentic if produced from proper custody. A document need not be authenticated if the opposing

201. Section 39 Superior Courts Act 10 of 2013 and Uniform Rule 38(3)–(8); ss 52, 53 Magistrates' Courts Act 32 of 1944 and Magistrates' Courts Rule 26(2).

202. These procedures are discussed in paras 158–165.

party has produced it and has been asked to put it before the court, when the court takes judicial notice of the document, or when the opposing party acknowledges its authenticity. A foreign document need not be authenticated before the court if it has been duly authenticated in its country of origin, or in accordance with the Hague Convention Abolishing the Requirement of Legalization for Foreign Public Documents.[203] A document that is not authenticated when this is required is inadmissible. Secondary evidence of the contents of a document is generally inadmissible. Some exceptions are when the document has been admitted, when the original is lost or destroyed or it is impossible to produce, when the original is in the possession of the opposing or a third party and he or she fails to produce it, or when a statutory exception exists.

291. In the Constitutional Court, a party to proceedings is entitled to canvass factual material that is relevant to the determination of the issues before the court and that does not appear on the record, in documents lodged with the registrar. Such facts must be common cause or otherwise incontrovertible, or must be of an official, scientific, technical or statistical nature and capable of easy verification. Other parties are permitted to respond to these documents.[204]

§5. Evidence in Small Claims Courts

292. Evidence in these courts is regulated statutorily.[205] The usual rules of the law of evidence do not apply, and a court may ascertain any relevant fact in such manner as it may consider fit. Evidence to prove or disprove any fact in issue may be submitted in writing or orally. The commissioner is required to proceed inquisitorially to ascertain the relevant facts and may question any party or witness at any stage of the proceedings. A party may not question or cross-examine any other party or any of their witnesses without permission of the court. While the Act does not specifically provide so, it is usual for the plaintiff to give viva voce evidence. The defendant may also give oral evidence in court and may, should he or she wish, lodge a written statement setting out his or her defence with the clerk of the court before the hearing. All parties are entitled to call witnesses. A court is empowered to decide that sufficient evidence has been led to reach a decision and to order that no further evidence may be adduced. Persons giving evidence must do so under oath, and provision is made for interpreters where necessary.

203. Uniform Rule 63 sets out this procedure.

204. Constitutional Court Rule 31; *see also* Constitutional Court Rule 29 which makes Uniform Rule 63 applicable to Constitutional Court proceedings.

205. *See* ss 26–28 Small Claims Courts Act 61 of 1984.

Part VIII. Particular Proceedings

293. Various proceedings do not conform to standard action or application procedures. The majority are not frequently used in practice and are therefore discussed very briefly. Interdicts are also dealt with here.

Chapter 1. Interdicts

294. An interdict is a remedy, not a procedure, and an existing application or an action procedure is used to obtain relief. An interdict is defined as a summary remedy of an extraordinary nature that protects a person against the unlawful deprivation of his or her rights. Three kinds of interdict exist: prohibitory interdicts, which are orders to abstain from committing or continuing a wrong; mandatory interdicts, which are orders compelling performance of a positive act; and restitutory interdicts, which restore possession of property.

295. Interdicts may be temporary or final in effect. A temporary interdict is granted on an interim basis and remains in force only until the rights of the parties have been canvassed before and decided by the court, while a final interdict is of permanent effect. For the grant of a final interdict, a party must show the following: a clear right established on a balance of probabilities; an actionable wrong already committed or a reasonable apprehension that such an act will be committed; and the absence of any other satisfactory remedy affording similar protection.[206] For the grant of a temporary interdict, the following requirements must be met: a clear right; alternatively, a right established only prima facie in which case the applicant must also show that he or she would suffer irreparable harm if the interdict were refused; the balance of convenience in favour of the grant of the interdict when the prejudice to each of the parties is considered; and the absence of any other satisfactory remedy.[207] The court must also recognize constitutional principles and, when weighing up the balance of convenience, consider the impact of the restraining order on any State organ against which an order is sought.[208]

296. The procedure followed depends on whether a material dispute of fact exists necessitating action procedure. Final interdicts are thus usually sought by way of action procedure, although application procedure may be used where the facts are not in dispute. Application procedure is always used to obtain a temporary interdict. If granted, such an interdict is only valid until action has been instituted to establish the rights of the parties, if a dispute of fact exists, until the application is finally determined, or until confirmation of the order on the return day. Confirmation of a temporary interdict gives it final effect; if it is discharged, it ceases to be of any effect.

297. Interdicts are also available in Magistrates' Courts, and the same general principles apply in these courts. They are not available in Small Claims Courts.

206. *Setlogelo v. Setlogelo* 1914 AD 221.
207. *Webster v. Mitchell* 1948 (1) SA 1186 (W); *Beecham Group Ltd v. B-M Group (Pty) Ltd* 1977 (1) SA 50 (T).
208. *National Treasury v. Opposition to Urban Tolling Alliance* 2012 (6) SA 223 (CC).

Chapter 2. Cases Where No Pleadings Are Filed

§1. Special Cases

298. Where parties to a dispute agree about the facts of the case but differ as to the legal conclusion that can be drawn from these facts, the parties may agree to make use of the special case procedure available in the High Court.[209] After proceedings have been instituted and it becomes apparent that the facts are not in issue, a written statement of facts in the form of a special case for the adjudication of the court is drafted by agreement between the parties. The statement consists of numbered paragraphs setting out the facts agreed on, the questions of law in dispute between the parties and their contentions thereon. Copies of any relevant documents must be attached. At the hearing, the court may make deductions of fact or law from the stated facts and documents as if proved at a trial.

§2. Questions of Law on Appeal

299. When the decision of an appeal from a single judge to a full bench depends exclusively on a point of law, the parties may agree to submit the decision to the court in the form of a special case, in which event copies must be made only of such portions of the record as may be necessary for a proper decision of the appeal. The court may, however, require to see the whole record. Similar provisions exist in respect of appeals to the Supreme Court of Appeal where the court may nevertheless order a full discussion of the case if it thinks fit.[210]

300. Where there is a conflict on a question of law between different High Courts, the Minister of Justice may submit the conflicting decisions to the Chief Justice, who must cause the matter to be argued before the Constitutional Court or the Supreme Court of Appeal.[211] The High Court will then be bound by that decision. No similar provisions exist in respect of appeals from lower courts.

209. Uniform Rule 33.
210. Uniform Rule 49(10); Supreme Court of Appeal Rule 8(8).
211. Section 20 Superior Courts Act 10 of 2013.

Chapter 3. Other Proceedings

§1. Interpleadre Proceedings

301. This procedure enables a person who is in possession of property that is not his or her own and that is claimed from him or her by two or more persons, to call on the rival claimants to appear before the court so that the right to such property may be determined. This procedure is most frequently used when the sheriff attaches property to be sold in execution and someone other than the judgment debtor makes claim to the property. The procedure to be followed is statutorily regulated and is available in both the High Court and Magistrates' Courts.[212]

§2. Declaration of Rights

302. At common law, a court would not determine the rights of parties in advance and would therefore not grant declaratory orders, while the Constitution only makes provision for a declaration of rights when a provision of the Bill of Rights has been infringed.[213] However, statutory provision exists for such orders, and Superior Courts may, in their discretion and at the instance of any interested person, enquire into and determine any existing, future or contingent right or obligation, despite the fact that the person cannot claim any consequential relief.[214] The right must not be one that may accrue in the future, but must be a present existing right that will only become enforceable at some future time. A declaration may be obtained either by issue of summons and the filing of ordinary pleadings, if the facts are in dispute or, if there is no dispute of fact, in the form of a special case after summons has been issued, or by means of motion proceedings. This procedure is not available in lower courts.

§3. De Lunatico Inquirendo

303. A specific form of ex parte application procedure is used when approaching the High Court for an order declaring persons of unsound mind, or of being incapable of managing their affairs, and appointing a curator to manage their affairs.[215]

212. Uniform Rule 58; Magistrates' Courts Rule 44.
213. Section 38 Constitution of the Republic of South Africa 1996.
214. Section 21(1)(c) Superior Courts Act 10 of 2013.
215. Uniform Rule 57.

§4. Perpetual Silence

304. In certain circumstances, a prospective litigant may be ordered to institute litigation within a specific time or be perpetually barred from doing so. Such an order may be requested if the applicant's rights are disturbed or interfered with by demands or threatened action; or if his or her reputation is suffering damage; or if a delay would prejudice the applicant's ability to defend the threatened action. The court has a discretion whether to grant the application and will consider factors such as the nature of the claim, the likelihood of prejudice and the balance of convenience. The court may also consider the possibility of testimony being lost owing to the death of witnesses or the loss of documents. This procedure is available only in the High Court.

§5. Vexatious Proceedings

305. A High Court may prohibit a specific person from instituting legal proceedings against any person in both superior and lower courts without the leave of the court concerned. Before it will grant such an order, the court must be satisfied that the person has persistently and without reasonable grounds repeatedly instituted litigation. The order may prohibit the institution of proceedings for an indefinite period or for such period as the court determines. Subsequent to such an order, a court will only grant leave to institute proceedings if satisfied that the intended proceedings are not an abuse of process, and that there are prima facie grounds for the proceedings.[216]

216. Vexatious Proceedings Act 3 of 1956.

Part IX. Preliminary Seizure and Enforcement of Judgments

Chapter 1. Preliminary Seizure

§1. Proceedings

I. Superior Courts

306. Preliminary seizure is not provided for by the Superior Courts Act or the Uniform Rules. However, our courts have held that it is within their inherent power to regulate their procedure in the interest of the proper administration of justice and therefore permit seizure in appropriate circumstances.[217] Preliminary seizure arises in two instances: first, an interim attachment of property to which the applicant claims a real or personal right to protect the right *pendente lite*, and second, where an applicant has a prima facie cause of action against the respondent and the respondent possesses vital evidence substantiating the cause of action that is liable to be destroyed unless the court makes an order for its preservation. In both instances, the attachment may be applied for ex parte and without notice if it is feared that the property or evidence will otherwise be destroyed or hidden. The respondent is protected to the extent that he or she may approach the court for an amendment of the interim order if he or she can show that the application was unjustified. The items subject to the interim attachment order are attached by the sheriff and retained in his or her custody pending a final determination.

II. Lower Courts

307. Section 30 of the Magistrates' Courts Act provides that these courts may grant orders for the attachment of things *pendente lite*. While various judgments have confirmed that interim attachment orders may be granted in respect of property to which the applicant claims a real or personal right, no clarity exists on whether a

217. *See Shoba v. Officer Commanding, Temporary Police Camp, Wagendrift Dam* 1995(4) SA 1 (A).

Magistrate's Court may attach evidence to safeguard it, as may be done in Superior Courts. Such an order is obtained by ex parte application, and the attached goods are retained by of the sheriff. If the property sought to be attached is the subject of an instalment sale transaction, the attachment must comply with provisions of the National Credit Act 34 of 2005. This Act requires the seller to require the debtor by letter to comply with his or her obligations in terms of the agreement within ten business days, and attachment may only be requested after expiry of this period. Section 32(1) of the Magistrates' Courts Act further provides that a lessor of premises may attach the lessee's movable property in security for payment of rent due. Security must be given by the lessor for any damages which the lessee might sustain should the attachment be set aside.

§2. Judicial Review

308. No specific provisions exist in either court for review of attachment orders. However, as such orders are not final, the respondent may always approach the court and request that the order be amended or set aside.

Chapter 2. Enforcement of Judgments

§1. Enforcement of Domestic Judgments

I. Proceedings

A. Superior Courts

309. The method used to enforce a judgment varies depending on the classification of the judgment. Judgments are classified as either *ad pecuniam solvendam* or *ad factum praestandum*. A judgment *ad pecuniam solvendam* is a judgment in which a debtor is ordered to pay a sum of money. It is immaterial in which area of law the claim arose (e.g., contract or delict); the only test is whether the judgment contains an order in money terms. A judgment *ad factum praestandum* is one where a person is ordered to perform, or refrain from performing, some action. Examples are orders for the transfer of immovable property, the delivery of movable property, and interdicts.

310. Judgments *ad pecuniam solvendam* are enforced by execution against the property of the debtor. The Abolition of Civil Imprisonment Act 2 of 1977 prohibits enforcement of such judgments against the person of a debtor. Movable and incorporeal property must always be attached first, and immovable property may only be attached if a *nulla bona* return has been made in respect of a writ against movable property or if, at the time of judgment, the court made a special order declaring specified immovable property executable. If the immovable property is the primary residence of the debtor, a writ may not be issued until the court has considered all relevant circumstances. Uniform Rule 45 provides that a writ of execution must be completed by the party in whose favour judgment has been given and then issued by the office of the registrar, either immediately after judgment or after taxation of any costs awarded, as such costs may only be recovered by writ after taxation. The writ is addressed to the sheriff, who must execute the judgment and furnish a return of service to both the court and the creditor. The sheriff must first demand satisfaction of the writ and, if the debtor is unable or unwilling to pay the amount due, may then proceed to attach property. When movable property is attached, it must immediately be inventoried and taken into the custody of the sheriff. The property is then sold by public auction to the highest bidder after advertisement of the sale. When immovable property is to be attached, the writ must contain a full description of the property. Attachment is effected by the sheriff serving a written notice on the owner of the property and the registrar of deeds. Notice must also be given to persons occupying the property. Preferent creditors and local authorities must be advised of any intended sale, and a preferent creditor may stipulate a reasonable reserve price for the sale. The property may be sold by public auction after various requirements concerning notice and advertisement have been met.[218]

218. Uniform Rules 45 and 46 contain full details of the procedure that must be followed when property is sold in execution.

Recent judgments have emphasized the need for the courts to consider all factors before granting such orders, as they limit the protection afforded by section 26 of the Constitution, which deals with access to adequate housing.[219] It should be noted that new amendments to the Rules of High Courts will now allow courts to set a 'reserve price' at which residential property of a defaulting home owner can be auctioned off.[220] Courts will now be able to set a minimum price at which bidding must commence, and they will consider factors such as *inter alia*, the market value of the property, the amount owed by the defaulting home owner in taxes and levies and the amount owed to banks. It is hoped that these amendments will provide justice for home owner defaulters.

311. Judgments *ad factum praestandum* are enforced by instituting proceedings for contempt of court. Contempt is a common law criminal offence and is committed whenever a wilful refusal to comply with a court order, whether civil or criminal, occurs. Although the State can prosecute any person who is alleged to have committed contempt, if the contempt relates to the failure to comply with a civil judgment, it is more usual for the creditor to approach the court that made the original order to obtain enforcement. This is done on notice of motion, requesting the court to commit the respondent to prison for contempt. For such an application to be successful, the applicant must show the following: the existence of an order *ad factum praestandum*; the defendant's knowledge of the order; his or her ability to comply with the order; and his or her wilful disobedience of the order. The court will usually impose a term of imprisonment but suspend its pending compliance with the original order. Maintenance orders are viewed as orders *ad factum praestandum* but are governed by the Maintenance Act 99 of 1998 which provides that non-compliance is a statutory offence.

B. Lower Courts

312. The Magistrates' Courts Act 32 of 1944 provides three different procedures relating to the enforcement of judgments. Apart from the usual execution procedure similar to that available in the Superior Courts, demand procedures, by which offers to settle debts can be enforced, and debt-collecting procedures are also available.[221] Demand procedures are only available in respect of liquidated claims. The two demand procedures are used after a letter of demand or summons has been issued, but before any further steps have been taken. Section 57 allows a debtor to admit liability and undertake to settle the debt in instalments coupled with a consent to judgment without

219. *See Jaftha v. Schoeman* 2005 (2) SA 140 (CC); *see also Gudwana v. Steko Development* 2011 (3) SA 608 (CC) and *Mkhize v. Umvoti Municipality* 2012 (1) SA (SCA).

220. *See* Uniform Rule 46A which addresses execution against residential immovable property. Also *see* Government Gazette 41257 No. 1272 dated 17 Nov. 2017. The new amendments come into effect on 22 Dec. 2017.

221. *See* ss 57, 58 and 65 for demand procedures, ss 66–70 for execution procedures and s. 65A–65M for debt-collecting procedures. *See also* s. 172(1) of the National Credit Act 34 of 2005 for instalment debts. Also *see* the introduction of new amendments to execution against residential immovable property in Magistrates' Courts Rule 43A. These amendments were introduced in Government Gazette 41257 No. 1272 dated 17 Nov. 2017. This rule is similar to the amendments in the High Courts discussed in para. 310 above.

notice, should he or she fail to pay as agreed. Section 58 provides for an immediate consent to judgment, usually coupled with an order to pay the debt in instalments. In terms of section 65, a debtor can also offer to pay the debt in instalments after judgment has been obtained; this offer is then made an order of court. The judgment is then an order to pay in specified instalments rather than to pay the full amount.

313. If a debtor fails to comply with an order in terms of any of these sections, or with any other order for payment of money, irrespective of whether the original claim was liquidated or not, the debt-collecting procedure created by section 65A may be used. This procedure is an inquiry into the debtor's financial position to ascertain how he or she can satisfy the judgment debt. During the proceedings the court obtains details of his or her financial position from the debtor and then determines what amount is available to be used to satisfy the debt each month. Committal for contempt may be ordered if the debtor fails to attend the proceedings. Provision is also made for the attachment of amounts owing to the debtor and for the attachment of a portion of his or her salary to satisfy the debt. The debt-collecting procedure can also be used for High Court judgments by filing a copy of the judgment and details of the amount still owing with the clerk of the relevant Magistrate's Court.

314. Provision is also made in section 74 for the debtor to apply for a modified form of insolvency if it becomes clear that he or she is not in a position to meet his or her financial obligations. The usual form of execution is also available in Magistrates' Courts and is substantially similar to what is said above in respect of Superior Courts.

315. After a judgment has been given in a Small Claims Court, the presiding officer is obliged to ask the debtor if he or she is able to satisfy the judgment immediately. If he or she is unable to do so, an inquiry into his or her financial position is held immediately. The court may then either authorize execution proceedings or order the debt to be paid in instalments.

II. Judicial Review

316. No specific provision is made for the review of execution or debt-collecting procedures in either superior or lower courts. However, various provisions afford a debtor some protection. Judgments become superannuated after three years, and if a creditor has not taken steps to recover the debt during this period, he or she may thereafter only do so with the leave of the court.[222] Any court that has issued a writ also has the power to set it aside on application by a party who must show 'good cause'. Provision is also made in both courts for interpleader proceedings, which enable a third party whose goods have been attached to prove his or her title to the property concerned.[223]

222. Uniform Rule 66(1); s. 63 Magistrates' Courts Act of 1944.
223. Uniform Rule 58; s. 69 Magistrates' Courts Act of 1944.

§2. Recognition and Enforcement of Foreign Judgments

317. No international treaties currently exist between South Africa and other countries by which the recognition and enforcement of foreign judgments are regulated. Although statutory provisions exist for the enforcement of foreign judgments, these provisions have seldom been utilized. Both the recognition and the enforcement of foreign judgments are therefore primarily regulated by common law principles.

I. Recognition

318. A court is asked to recognize a foreign judgment when it is required to accept, but not enforce, the judgment. A foreign judgment is therefore recognized when the court concludes that the matter has been finally decided and need not be litigated further. All judgments must be recognized before enforcement can take place, but numerous judgments (e.g., those affecting status) only require recognition, not enforcement. Two principal requirements must be met for recognition. The first is that the judgment must have been given by a court whose jurisdiction is deemed competent by the rules of South African private international law; that is, the court must have had the power to bring the parties before it and to decide upon the matters with which it dealt. The second is that the judgment must be final and conclusive in its own forum.

II. Enforcement

319. Only the enforcement of claims sounding in money will be dealt with, as enforcement of claims relating to status and property require the consideration of private international law concepts, which cannot be dealt with adequately within the scope of this work. As mentioned above, enforcement can, in theory, take place either in terms of the common law or in terms of a statute.

III. Enforcement at Common Law

320. This is currently the only practicable method of enforcing a foreign judgment other than judgments emanating from some neighbouring States. Before a judgment can be enforced, certain general prerequisites must be met. Four such prerequisites have been identified by our courts and writers. The first is that the rendering court must have competent jurisdiction under the principles of South African private international law. The opinion of the foreign court as to its competence to exercise jurisdiction is not relevant. The courts have not set general guidelines and have recognized or refused recognition in the particular circumstances of each case. However, certain rules have crystallized, and a foreign court will be deemed to have had jurisdiction if the defendant was domiciled or resident in that country when the original action was instituted or had submitted to the jurisdiction of the court. Citizenship or the attachment of property does not confer jurisdiction. It is debatable whether casual presence in a country or the fact that the cause of action arose there will be viewed by a South African court as vesting that country's court with jurisdiction. The second prerequisite is that the judgment must be final: it must conclusively establish the existence of the debt so as to make it res judicata between the parties. This does not mean that the judgment may not be open to appeal or review proceedings, and enforcement may be sought even if the time limits for noting appeal have not prescribed, although it is probable that if an appeal is actually in progress, the court will suspend enforcement until the outcome is known. Third, the judgment must not be superannuated and therefore no longer capable of enforcement in the rendering country. A time limitation in the foreign country cannot be circumvented by enforcement in South Africa. Finally, the judgment must be for a definite sum of money or sufficiently fixed that all that is necessary to make it definite is a simple arithmetical calculation. The date of original judgment is the date on which any rate of exchange must be calculated. If the above four requirements have been met, a foreign judgment is enforceable unless the defendant can raise a valid defence. As the merits of the original action are not considered, the only defences that can be raised are that the judgment was obtained by fraud or that it is contrary to public policy or natural justice. The procedure for enforcement in terms of the common law is circuitous and direct enforcement (i.e., by registration) is not possible. A fresh action must be instituted in South Africa and the foreign judgment, duly authenticated through diplomatic channels, is merely viewed as a cause of action. Action must be instituted in either the High Court or the Magistrate's Court depending on the amount claimed. The judgment is then one given by a competent South African court, and the full range of debt-collecting procedures is available to the plaintiff should the defendant fail to comply with the judgment.

IV. Statutory Enforcement

321. The Enforcement of Foreign Civil Judgments Act 32 of 1988 came into effect in August 1990, and in theory statutory enforcement is now possible. However, this Act requires the Minister of Justice to designate certain countries to whose judgments the Act will apply, and this has not occurred to date. Reciprocal agreements have been concluded with the Republics of Namibia and Zimbabwe, and once these countries have adopted municipal legislation concerning enforcement of foreign judgments in their territories, they will become designated countries for purposes of this Act. The provisions of the Act are set out nevertheless for the sake of completeness. Section 1 provides that only final judgments for the payment of money in civil proceedings that are enforceable by execution in the country in which they are made may be enforced. Judgments for the payment of taxes, fines or other penalties and maintenance payments are specifically excluded. Maintenance payments are, however, covered by a separate Act, the Reciprocal Enforcement of Maintenance Orders Act 80 of 1963, which provides for the reciprocal enforcement of maintenance orders made in South Africa and in certain proclaimed countries. The statutory procedure is faster and more streamlined than the common law counterpart. A copy of the judgment, certified as a true copy in the rendering country, must be lodged at the South African Magistrate's Court where the defendant resides, carries on business or owns property. The clerk of this court registers the judgment for the amount payable, interest, and the costs of registration. A notice to the defendant is then issued and served on him or her by a court official. The defendant is afforded twenty-one days to pay the amount set out in the notice, failing which execution procedures may be instituted against him or her. Because the Act provides for the direct enforcement of judgments, the validity of the foreign judgment is not considered before its registration in South Africa. There are no prerequisites. However, the Act provides for the setting aside of registered judgments in circumstances that approximate the common law requirements and defences. A judgment may be set aside if the court in the rendering country had no jurisdiction to hear the matter. A court is deemed to have jurisdiction if the defendant was resident in that country, or in the case of juristic persons, had an office there. In addition, a court will have jurisdiction if a defendant voluntarily appears before it or agrees to submit to its jurisdiction. In actions relating to immovable property, the property must be situated in that country. Judgments may also be set aside if: the defendant did not receive notice of the proceedings and did not appear before the court; the judgment was obtained by fraud; enforcement of the judgment would be contrary to South African public policy; the matter in dispute has been subject to a prior final judgment; the judgment has been set aside by a competent court; the judgment has prescribed or been satisfied; or the judgment may not be recognized or enforced in terms of South African legislation. As stated earlier, it must be borne in mind that, although this procedure is faster and easier than the common law procedure, it cannot be used as no countries have yet been designated in terms of the Act.

Part X. Arbitration

Chapter 1. Arbitrability

322. Arbitration refers to a process in terms of which the parties to a dispute voluntarily and jointly ask a third party, the arbitrator, to hear both sides of their dispute and make an award that they undertake in advance will be accepted as final and binding. The fact that the arbitrator settles the dispute by making a legally binding award distinguishes arbitration from mediation and negotiation. For this reason, arbitration is more similar to litigation, as both are command processes where a decision is imposed on the parties, in contrast to negotiation and mediation, which are consensual in nature. But, in contrast to litigation, the arbitrator's award arises from the consent of the parties to accept the award, not from the power of the court to impose an order.

323. The South African Constitution's Bill of Rights provides that 'everyone has the right to have any dispute that can be resolved by the application of law decided in a fair public hearing before a court or, where appropriate, another independent and impartial tribunal or forum'. The Supreme Court of Appeal has held that it is debatable whether this section applies to private arbitration proceedings, as the parties can exclude any form of public hearing, but that, even if the fairness requirement in this section does apply to such proceedings, the parties can themselves define what is fair.

324. The four distinctive attributes of arbitration are that: it proceeds from an agreement between parties who consent to a process by which an arbitrator reaches a decision that is binding on the parties; the agreement provides for a process whereby the substantive rights of the parties are determined; the arbitrator is chosen by the parties or by a method to which they have consented; the rights of the parties are determined in an impartial manner in respect of a dispute which is formulated at the time that the arbitrator is appointed.

325. Arbitration can take place in terms of the common law, in terms of the Arbitration Act 42 of 1965, or in terms of one of the statutes that provide for compulsory arbitration. The best known of these are the Labour Relations Act 66 of 1995 for employer/employee disputes, the Land Affairs Act 101 of 1987 for expropriation compensation payments, and various expropriation ordinances.

326. Common law arbitration derives from Roman law as developed by Roman-Dutch jurists. Unlike arbitration under the Arbitration Act, parties need not agree to arbitration in writing; a verbal agreement suffices. It is also unnecessary for the parties to comply with the provisions of the Act when reaching agreement or during proceedings. If common law awards are not complied with voluntarily, they must be enforced by obtaining a subsequent court order.

327. Matrimonial matters and matters incidental thereto may not be referred to arbitration in terms of the Act. Matters relating to status (e.g., legitimacy and mental capacity) are also not subject to arbitration.[224] Criminal cases may not be referred to arbitration. If the dispute relates to the validity of the contract containing the arbitration agreement, the matter may also not be referred to arbitration.

224. Section 2 Arbitration Act 42 of 1965.

Chapter 2. Arbitration Agreement and Party Autonomy

328. The Act defines an arbitration agreement as a written agreement providing for the reference to arbitration of any existing or future dispute relating to a matter specified in the agreement, whether an arbitrator is named or designated therein or not.[225] The agreement is a contract and is subject to the law of contract. All the requirements for the conclusion of a valid contract must be met. As the arbitration agreement is embodied in a contract, which may be drafted to suit the parties' specific requirements, the statements that follow must all be read as general principles that may be amended by the parties to the agreement. The parties must also have contractual capacity. Agreements that are not in writing are regulated by the common law, not the Act. Arbitration clauses may be incorporated into other contracts and will then constitute agreements under the Act. Such clauses may be limited or of a universal character.

329. An arbitration agreement may only be terminated with the consent of all the parties thereto. A High Court may, however, set an arbitration agreement aside in certain circumstances. It is not terminated by the death or insolvency of one of the parties. If legal proceedings are instituted by a party in respect of a matter that it was agreed would be referred to arbitration, the court may stay such proceedings if satisfied that there is no good reason why the dispute should not be referred to arbitration.

330. The parties control the arbitration process and may select an arbitrator with mutually acceptable expertise, choose the rules of arbitration that he or she must apply, determine the issues that will be submitted for arbitration and arrange the venue and date for the proceedings.

225. Sections 3 and 6 Arbitration Act 42 of 1965.

Chapter 3. Composition of Arbitral Tribunal

331. Parties to the agreement may appoint whomever they wish to act as arbitrator.[226] Any reference is to a single arbitrator unless the agreement provides otherwise. An arbitrator is not the agent of the party who appointed him or her and must act impartially. If an arbitrator refuses to act or is no longer capable of acting due to death or incapacity, the party who appointed him or her may appoint another arbitrator. If an agreement provides for an even number of arbitrators, the arbitrators may at any time appoint an umpire, who then has the sole power to decide the dispute unless the agreement provides otherwise. A High Court also has the power to appoint an arbitrator or umpire when a party fails to do so or when the parties cannot agree on an appointment.

332. The appointment of an arbitrator cannot be terminated except by consent of all the parties. Two exceptions to this rule apply. First, the arbitration agreement may provide otherwise and, second, the court may at any time on the application of any party, on good cause shown, set aside the appointment of an arbitrator. The expression 'good cause' includes failure on the part of the arbitrator or umpire to use all reasonable speed in commencing and proceeding with the arbitration and making an award or, in a case where two arbitrators are unable to agree, in giving notice of that fact to the parties. Where the appointment of an arbitrator is set aside, the court may, apart from any order for costs which may be awarded against such arbitrator personally, order that such arbitrator will not be entitled to any remuneration for his or her services.

226. *See* in general ss 9–13 Arbitration Act 42 of 1965.

Chapter 4. Interim Measures and Preliminary Awards

333. If a party to an arbitration agreement commences court proceedings against any other party to the agreement, in respect of any matter agreed to be referred to arbitration, the latter party may apply to the court for a stay of such proceedings. If the court is satisfied that there is no good reason why the dispute should not be referred to arbitration, the court may make an order suspending the court proceedings, subject to such terms and conditions as it may consider just. The court has a discretion not to refer the matter to arbitration but to allow it to proceed in a court of law. If the matter is one which cannot be settled by arbitration, for example, if the validity of the agreement is challenged, the matter will in any case not be referred to arbitration.

334. Unless the arbitration agreement provides otherwise, the arbitration tribunal may make an interim award at any time within the period allowed for making an award.

Chapter 5. Conduct of Arbitral Proceedings

335. All parties must be given written notice of the time and venue of the proceedings.[227] Every party is entitled to be present and to be heard either personally or through a representative. If a party has received notice but fails to attend without good cause, the tribunal may proceed in his or her absence. Persons may be subpoenaed to give evidence and to produce books and documents in the same manner as in a civil trial. The parties may determine the manner of and extent to which the evidence of witnesses should be recorded.

The Act provides that a tribunal may: determine the time and place of proceedings; administer the oath; examine the parties and other persons who have been summoned to give evidence; require production of books and documents; and inspect property involved in the reference. It may also, on application of one of the parties: require a party to make discovery and produce documents; require a party to file pleadings or statements of claim and defence; require a party to allow inspection of property; appoint a commissioner to take evidence outside South Africa.

Where two arbitrators constitute a tribunal, their unanimous decision is the decision of the tribunal. Where a tribunal consists of more than two arbitrators, the majority decision is the tribunal's decision. If a majority decision cannot be reached and written notice thereof is given, an umpire must take the place of the tribunal and has the powers of a sole arbitrator.

Before a final award is made, a tribunal may, on application by a party or by agreement between the parties, state any question of law in the form of a special case for the opinion of the High Court or of an advocate. Such an opinion is binding on the tribunal.

336. A High Court has certain general powers in relation to tribunal procedure. It may make orders in respect of security for costs, discovery of documents, examination of witnesses before commissioners, giving of evidence by affidavit, inspection, interim custody and preservation of property, interim interdicts, securing the amount in dispute, and appointment of a receiver. Non-compliance with many of the above provisions constitutes an offence.

---

227. *See* ss 14–17, 22 Arbitration Act 42 of 1965.

Chapter 6. Arbitral Award

337. The powers of an arbitrator are usually set out in the arbitration agreement.[228] Although the Act accords certain powers to arbitration tribunals, these may be varied by the agreement. However, arbitrators cannot make an award that is not founded on the arbitration agreement and can therefore only impose duties and confer rights that flow from the agreement.

338. Subject to the provisions of the Act, an award is final and not subject to appeal. The parties must comply with the award in accordance with its terms. An award must address all the issues in dispute and constitute a complete, certain and final determination of all the matters referred to arbitration. An incomplete award may be referred back to the arbitrator by a court for a full decision. An award that goes beyond its terms of reference will have those portions deleted. Unless the agreement provides otherwise, an arbitrator must make an award within four months after commencing an inquiry into the case or being called on to act by any party, whichever is the earlier date. Where an umpire has been called on to act, an award must be made within three months. The parties may by agreement, or the court may on good cause shown, extend these times. The award must be in writing and signed by the tribunal. It must be delivered in the presence of the parties or after they have been summoned to appear. It is deemed to have been made known to the parties on the day of delivery. Interim orders may also be made and specific performance of a contract ordered in circumstances in which a court could do so. If payment of money is ordered, the sum carries interest from the date of the award.

339. Within six weeks after publication of an award, the parties may by agreement, or the court may on application, remit any matter which was referred to arbitration back to the tribunal for reconsideration and the making of a further award or a fresh award. The matter must be disposed of by the tribunal within three months.

228. *See* in general ss 23–33 Arbitration Act 42 of 1965.

Chapter 7. Recourse Against Arbitral Award

340. On application by any of the parties, the High Court may set aside an award in the following instances: where an arbitrator has misconducted himself or herself in relation to his or her arbitration duties, by acting in a wrongful or improper way; where an arbitrator has committed a gross irregularity in the conduct of the proceedings; where an arbitrator has exceeded his or her powers by going beyond his or her terms of reference; or where an award has been improperly obtained. Such applications must be made within six weeks after publication of the award except when requested on the grounds of corruption. If an award is set aside, the dispute must be submitted to a new tribunal at the request of any of the parties.

Chapter 8. Recognition and Enforcement of Awards

341. The award may be made an order of court on application by either party and then enforced in the same manner as any judgment or order. A court will not enforce an arbitration award that sanctions an illegality.[229] The International Arbitration Act 15 of 2017 has recently been introduced as per Government Gazette 41347 of 20 December 2017. It came into effect on 20 December 2017. It addresses *inter alia*, the use of arbitration as a method of resolving international commercial disputes, the adoption of the Model Law for use in international commercial disputes and the recognition and enforcement of certain arbitration agreements and arbitral awards. It repeals the Recognition and Enforcement of Foreign Awards Act of 1977.

229. *Cool Ideas 1186 CC v. Hubbard* [2014] ZACC 16.

Part XI. Mediation

Chapter 1. Legislation/Definitions

342. Prior to December 2014, all mediation was voluntary and non-legislated. Various organizations exist that regulate mediators and training of mediators. Such mediation is defined as a private, voluntary, and consensual process whereby parties attempt to resolve their differences.

343. From 1 December 2014, an additional form of mediation, court-annexed mediation, has become available on a trial basis in various Magistrates' Courts. The purpose of such mediation is described as to promote access to justice and restorative justice, to preserve relationships between litigants which may become strained or destroyed by the adversarial nature of litigation, to facilitate an expeditious and cost-effective resolution of a dispute, to assist litigants to determine at an early stage whether proceeding with a trial is in their best interests, and finally, to provide litigants with solutions to their dispute which are beyond the scope and powers of judicial officers. The Magistrates' Courts rules have been amended by the insertion of new rules to regulate this procedure. These rules define mediation as the process by which a mediator assists the parties in actual or potential litigation to resolve the dispute between them by facilitating discussion between the parties, assisting them in identifying issues, clarifying priorities, exploring areas of compromise, and generating options in an attempt to resolve the dispute.

Chapter 2. Rights That Can Be Subject to Mediation

344. Any matter may be subject to voluntary mediation, as this is solely dependent on the consent of the parties to the mediation process. The rules for court-annexed mediation provide that any civil dispute may be referred to mediation.

Chapter 3. Mediation Agreement

345. Parties to voluntary mediation may contractually bind themselves to undergo this process in the event of any dispute. Court-annexed mediation may be requested by any party both prior to and after the commencement of litigation. The other party must agree to submit the dispute to mediation. If he or she agrees, a mediation agreement is concluded which deals with details of the mediation sessions and the consequences of a party not abiding by the agreement. During the course of litigation, the court may also enquire into the possibility of mediation and grant the parties an opportunity to refer the dispute to a court official to facilitate mediation.

Chapter 4. Persons/Institutions That Can Act as Mediator

346. In general terms, all that is required from a mediator in voluntary mediation proceedings is that he or she must be impartial and accepted by the parties, and that his or her actions be fair and unprejudiced. A mediator need not be a lawyer; social worker, psychologist or anyone else who has been trained as such may act as mediator. Court-annexed mediation may only be performed by accredited mediators, and anyone who wishes to offer such services must attend training courses in compliance with the norms and standards set by the Minister of Justice.

Chapter 5. Mediation Procedure

347. There is no prescribed procedure for voluntary mediation, and the parties are free to create a procedure that suits their own convenience. In court-annexed mediation, the parties may select an accredited mediator, themselves determine the date, time, and venue of mediation, the time within which mediation will be concluded and the confidentiality and privilege attaching to disclosures during mediation. After the mediation agreement has been concluded, the party claiming relief must lodge a statement of claim with the registrar of court within ten days of signature, while the party against whom relief is claimed must lodge a statement of defence within ten days of receipt of the statement of claim. At the commencement of mediation proceedings, the mediator is obliged to inform the parties about the purpose of mediation and its objectives. He or she must also explain the rules that will apply to the mediation. No further procedures are prescribed. The mediator's fees must be borne equally between the parties to mediation.

Chapter 6. Settlement Agreement

348. In voluntary mediation, a settlement agreement is dependent on the consent of the parties and cannot be enforced by the mediator. For this reason, it is non-binding on the parties and, at most, could be legally enforced in terms of the law of contract. In court-annexed mediation, if the parties reach a settlement, an agreement must be drafted and filed with the registrar of the court. This agreement must be in writing and signed by the parties. If litigation has not commenced, the registrar merely files the settlement agreement. If litigation has already commenced, a judicial officer will note that the dispute has been resolved and may make the agreement an order of court.

Chapter 7. Setting Aside a Settlement Agreement

349. In voluntary mediation, a settlement agreement will require the institution of litigation to have it set aside, should only one party wish to set it aside. In court-annexed mediation, if a settlement agreement has been made an order of court, it will require an appeal or review to have it set aside.

Chapter 8. International Mediation

350. No provision is made in court-annexed mediation for international mediation.

Selected Bibliography

This bibliography comprises only the most recent publications in the field of procedure and publications that appear in looseleaf format or that have yearly supplements to ensure that the information is up-to-date. Reference to other publications on specific topics will be found in the footnotes to the text.

Constitutional Court and Superior Courts

Cilliers, A.C., C. Loots & H.C. Nel. *Herbstein and van Winsen The Civil Practice of the High Courts and the Supreme Court of Appeal of South Africa.* 5th ed. Cape Town, South Africa: Juta, 2009.

Erasmus, H.J. *Superior Court Practice.* 1st ed. Cape Town, South Africa: Juta, 1994 (looseleaf update 2014).

Lower Courts

Van Loggerenberg, D.E. *Jones and Buckle: The Civil Practice of the Magistrates' Courts in South Africa.* 10th ed. Cape Town, South Africa: Juta, 1997, 2011.

General

Harms, D.R. 'Civil Procedure: High Court'. In *Law of South Africa.* Vol. 4, 3rd ed. Founding editor W.A. Joubert. Durban, South Africa: Butterworths, 2012.

Cilliers, A.C. 'Costs'. Revised by M Carnelley. In *Law of South Africa.* Vol. 3, Part 2, 2nd ed. Founding editor W.A. Joubert. Durban, South Africa: Butterworths, 2006.

Dendy, M. 'Jurisdiction'. In *Law of South Africa.* Vol. 11, 2nd ed. Founding editor W.A. Joubert. Durban, South Africa: Butterworths, 2008.

Paleker, M. 'Civil Procedure: Magistrates' Courts'. In *Law of South Africa.* Vol. 5, 3rd ed. Founding editor W.A. Joubert. Durban, South Africa: Butterworths, 2013.

Jivan, U.A. 'Judicial Officers'. In *Law of South Africa.* Vol. 11, 2nd ed. Founding editor W.A. Joubert. Durban, South Africa: Butterworths, 2008.

McQuoid-Mason, D.J. 'Legal Aid'. In *Law of South Africa.* Vol. 14, Part 2, 2nd edn. Founding editor W.A. Joubert. Durban, South Africa: Butterworths, 2007.

Schmidt, C.W.H. & D.T. Zeffertt. 'Evidence'. Updated by D.P. van der Merwe. In *Law of South Africa.* Vol. 9, 2nd ed. Founding editor W.A. Joubert. Durban, South Africa: Butterworths, 2005.

Butler, D.W. (Original text by Smith, C.) 'Arbitration'. *Law of South Africa.* Vol. 1 2nd ed. Founding editor W.A. Joubert. Durban, South Africa: Butterworths, 2003.

van Dijkhorst, K. 'Courts'. In *Law of South Africa.* Vol. 5, Part 2, 2nd ed. Founding editor W.A. Joubert. Durban, South Africa: Butterworths, 2004.

van Dijkhorst, K. & J. Church. 'Legal Practitioners'. In *Law of South Africa.* Vol. 14, Part 2, 2nd ed. Founding editor W.A. Joubert. Durban, South Africa: Butterworths, 2007.

Index

The numbers here refers to paragraph numbers.

Index

Made in the USA
Monee, IL
18 October 2026

66037590R10083